THE EDUCATION OF MAN

The Educational Philosophy of
JACQUES MARITAIN

Edited, with an Introduction, by
DONALD *and* IDELLA GALLAGHER

Boston College

Library of Congress Cataloging in Publication Data

Maritain, Jacques, 1882-1973.
  The education of man.

  Reprint of the 1967 ed. published by the University
of Notre Dame Press, Notre Dame, Ind.
  Bibliography: p.
  1. Education--Philosophy. I. Gallagher, Donald A.
II. Gallagher, Idella J. III. Title.
[LB775.M3566 1976]   370.1   75-28667
ISBN 0-8371-8479-7

This edition originally published in 1976 by University
of Notre Dame Press, South Bend, Ind.

Reprinted with the permission of Doubleday & Company, Inc.

Reprinted in 1976 by Greenwood Press,
a division of Williamhouse-Regency Inc.

Library of Congress Catalog Card Number 75-28667

ISBN 0-8371-8479-7

Printed in the United States of America

Grateful acknowledgment herewith is made to the following for permission to reprint the material listed below.

The Preface to *Philosophy and Education* by Franz de Hovre, translated by Edward B. Jordan, reprinted with the permission of the publishers, Benziger Brothers, Inc., New York.

"The Conquest of Freedom" from *Freedom: Its Meaning*, edited by Ruth Nanda Anshen, copyright 1940 by Harcourt, Brace & World, Inc.

"The Education of Women" from the Address, *The Inauguration* of *George N. Schuster, The Fifth President*, 1941, by Jacques Maritain. Reprinted by permission of Hunter College of the City University of New York.

Excerpts from the *National Society for the Study of Education's 54th Yearbook*. Reprinted by permission.

"Moral Education" by Jacques Maritain, from *A College Goes to School: Centennial Lectures*. Reprinted by permission of St. Mary's College, Indiana.

"Education and the Humanities" by Jacques Maritain, Centenary Lecture delivered at St. Michael's College, Toronto, 1952. Reprinted by permission of the author and St. Michael's College.

"Moral and Spiritual Values in Education" by Jacques Maritain, from the Proceedings of the Eighty-ninth Convocation of the Board of Regents of the State of New York. Reprinted by permission of the New York State Education Department.

The excerpts from *Education at the Crossroads* by Jacques Maritain, in Chapter 2, "Thomist Views on Education." "Some Typical Aspects of Christian Education" by Jacques Maritain, from *The Christian Idea of Education*, edited by Edmund Fuller, copyright © 1957 by the Kent School Corporation. Both reprinted by permission of Yale University Press.

"Education for the Good Life" by Jacques Maritain from the April 26, 1946, issue of *The Commonweal*, the weekly journal of opinion edited by Catholic laymen. Reprinted by permission.

ACKNOWLEDGMENTS

We wish to express our gratitude to the Very Reverend Robert Russell, O.S.A., Chairman of the Philosophy Department of Villanova University for his friendly encouragement of this project, and to our graduate assistants (1960–62) who aided in various phases of the work, particularly Mr. Donald Inverso. To Mrs. Helen Stoughton go our thanks for assisting with the typing of the manuscript. We are grateful above all to Professor Maritain for his advice and constant inspiration.

TABLE OF CONTENTS

INTRODUCTION

Toward a Christian Philosophy of Education

"Teaching is an art; the teacher is an artist." Jacques Maritain, who will be remembered as one of the great and inspiring teachers of our day, devoted himself unsparingly to this art for almost fifty years at the Collège Stanislas and the Institut Catholique in Paris, at the Institute of Mediaeval Studies in Toronto, at Princeton University in the United States, and, as visiting professor, at many other universities both in America and abroad. The philosophy of education issuing from this half century of teaching, and from meditating upon the principles of education and the practical problems involved in schooling the young, is undoubtedly one of the lasting contributions of this eminent Thomist to twentieth-century thought.

Maritain is well known for his original and sometimes controversial ideas in fields that are specifically philosophical. He is also known for his provocative ideas in the frontier regions where philosophy borders on other disciplines. The fruits of his pioneering work in the philosophy of art, for example, are *Art and Scholasticism* (1922) and *Creative Intuition in Art and Poetry* (1953). And just as there is no philosophy of art in the formal sense, so there is no explicit philosophy of education in the writings of St. Thomas.[1] Among the contemporary thinkers engaged in the development of such a philosophy, Maritain occupies a leading place. In *Education at the Crossroads* (1943) and in the studies contained in the present volume, he has drawn the outlines of a Christian philosophy of education for our time.

Any educational philosophy worthy of the name is, quite simply, both a theory and a program—a theory of what the education of man for freedom ought to be, and a program for achieving this goal. As Maritain states in Chapter II, "Education directed toward wisdom, and centered on the humanities, aiming to develop in people the capacity to think correctly and to enjoy truth and beauty, is education for freedom, or liberal education."[2] All of the writings of Jacques Maritain on the subject of education are attempts to develop the full implications of this statement. By freedom in this context he does not mean freedom from constraint, or mere animal spontaneity, but freedom in a more profound sense, that freedom of autonomy or expansion about which he has written so luminously. This *terminal freedom*, as he calls it, is the fulfillment of the deepest potentialities of the human being. And while it is fully attainable only in and through God, there are in this life analogous though imperfect realizations of it in the spiritual, intellectual, and moral life of man. "The Conquest of Freedom" (Chapter VIII of this volume) is Maritain's most comprehensive treatment of this theme and one of the most original statements of the Thomist philosophy of freedom.

Education is "the pursuit of truth to make men free."[3] The ideas of truth, freedom, and man are so closely bound up with one another that we must grasp their interrelationships if we are to achieve a right understanding of the education of man. "There is no other foundation for the educational task," says Maritain, "than the eternal saying: It is truth which sets man free."[4] Every philosopher, classical or modern, who belongs to the humanistic tradition declares that his aim is—and how could he claim anything else?—the teaching of truth in order to set man free. Without harking back to Plato, Aristotle, Augustine, Aquinas, and the other great educators of antiquity and of the Middle Ages, we need only recall that Maritain's collaborators in the *Fifty-fourth Yearbook of the National Society for the Study of Education,* men professing such diverse philosophies as Pragmatism, Realism, Christian Idealism, and Existentialism, make similar claims. Even Marxists and Pragmatists, who repudiate liberal education in the traditional sense, maintain that their educational program is "humanizing" and will liberate man.[5]

What matters, evidently, is how the philosopher answers the questions "What is man? Truth? Freedom?" and how in the light of these answers he conceives the aims, the content, and the order of education? It is not a question of pitting the old methods against the new, or of labeling this or that theory illiberal because it does not always follow traditional patterns. The fundamental issue is well stated by John Dewey to be not that of "new versus old education, not of progressive against traditional education, but a question of what anything whatsoever must be to be worthy of the name of education."[6]

Maritain would agree that we must dispense with labels and inquire into the meaning of education itself, but for him there is no true education which is not humanistic; to speak of "education and the humanities" is to speak of "education and education." In his writings on education he brings out in vigorous and precise language the doctrines of perennial philosophy, and in particular those of St. Thomas, on man and freedom, and shows in terms of these doctrines what sort of education the human person living in a free society is entitled to receive. At the same time he insists that there is a good deal to be learned from contemporary psychiatry, psychology, and philosophy, for example, about the psychosomatic unity of man, a truth stressed by Aristotle but neglected or distorted by many philosophers of early modern times. There is also much to be learned about method, he

believes, from progressive education and other educational theories of the present day.[7]

Both the progressivist-experimentalists and the Marxists assail the type of liberal education which revolves around a study of the Greek and Latin classics or the great books of the Western tradition. Such an education, they say, is a narrow concentration upon supposedly immutable values, or else a bourgeois glorification of the spectator ideal of leisure. They point to the ancient and medieval periods, when the few luxuriated in the contemplation of beauty and truth while the slaves or serfs did the work. They point to the aristocratic and bourgeois societies of modern times, in which, they say, the gentlemen enjoy art and culture while the proletarians labor and produce all the wealth.[8]

Jacques Maritain does not reject such criticisms altogether. Like John Dewey, he also repudiates the kind of contemplation and leisure which consists in the epicurean enjoyment that a "cultivated" spectator might derive from observing the spectacle of life, and from savoring its rarer moments. Of this ideal, George Santayana is the exquisite embodiment. Maritain regards this hedonistic transmutation as a degradation and a denaturing of true contemplation. Likewise, he insists that the kind of liberal and humanistic education he is advocating ought not to be confused with the various types of liberal education prevalent in the modern period from the sixteenth to the nineteenth centuries. This so-called liberal education has often been dominated by a rationalistic philosophy animated by the Cartesian passion for clear and distinct ideas.

THE SOCIAL AND CULTURAL CONTEXT OF EDUCATION

When the social and cultural features of the early modern period are contrasted with those of the present day, it becomes evident why the type of education suited for that age can no longer be satisfactory. Comparing the ways in which liberal education was conceived in the past and must now be looked upon today, Maritain stresses three points: (1) Until comparatively recent times, education was regarded as the privilege of the few. Even in Christian countries the practical and social applications of the notion of man as a person with a spiritual soul and with inalienable rights were unconsciously restricted. At the present time democratic thought, in spite of the many shortcomings of democratic societies, has made undeniable progress. The discrepancy between the implications of the metaphysical idea of man as a person, and the social applications of this idea, has been eliminated in principle, even though obviously not always in practice. It follows that liberal education can no longer be confined to the privileged few but must be made available to all. (2) The most important of the secondary aims of education in the past was the preparation of the youth of the upper class for the responsibilities of government. Nowadays the most essential of the secondary aims must be the preparation of all youth for active citizenship. (3) In the previous age, knowledge was of high quality but comparatively small in quantity. "It was possible for a man not only to be genuinely cultivated in all of them [the liberal disciplines] but also to master creatively a variety of them, so as to attain the very level of intellectual virtues in his approach to universal knowledge." In the past century, there has been an enormous increase in the amount of knowledge with which education must concern itself. "Universal knowledge," says Maritain, "remains the ideal goal of education, but no man can henceforth, in his approach to universal knowledge, hope to develop the various intellectual virtues and intellectual skills necessary to master creatively its various fields."[9]

It is significant that men like Dewey, Maritain, and Whitehead, who are poles apart in their philosophical thinking, would find themselves in agreement on many points of their analysis and criticism of traditional patterns of education, and even in many of their constructive proposals for reform. They disagree in their fundamental understanding of what man's nature is and in a number of the objectives of education.[10]

Maritain's great interest in the social and cultural context of education is evidenced in his statement that "the most crucial problem with which our educational system is confronted is one of civilization."[11] Just as there is an intimate bond between education and civilization, so, too, educational philosophy and the philosophy of culture or civilization are closely related. Jacques Maritain is one of the few Thomist thinkers who have devoted attention to the vitally important area of the philosophy of culture. In "Education and the Good Life," the relationship between culture and education is clearly brought out. "The crucial need for modern education is to free itself from the background of this philosophy [positivism and pragmatism] which is but a hindrance to its inspiration and which takes the edge off the sense of truth and off the eternal values of our minds. . . . But the very choice of that road of real progress and emancipation will indispensably require that the new age of civilization abandon in all fields, and especially in the field of education, a philosophy of life which disarms and jeopardizes the highest powers of man, and that it find anew, in a heroic manner, faith in truth, in reason, and in God. . . . What we need first of all is a renewal both of metaphysics and of morality, backed up by faith in the Gospel. This is true in the general field of culture; it is especially true in the field of education."[12]

Maritain does not distinguish culture and civilization as do certain sociologists and anthropologists. Culture, or civilization, is the expansion of the human life and includes not only a sufficient measure of material development but also the development "of the speculative and practical activities (artistic and ethical) peculiarly worthy of being called a human development."[13]

It is evident from these texts that the school ought to assist in the cultivation of the human being. In this perspective of the philosophy of culture, and the analysis of the cultural and social features of various epochs, the distinguishing characteristics of Maritain's educational philosophy stand out. It is a philosophy fed by the springs of Christian wisdom but also quickened by vital contact with the social reality of our time. Before touching upon the distinctive aspects of his philosophy of education, however, let us recall Maritain's remarks on the "crucial problem of the education of the human being." Our age affords a rare opportunity for true education in which all men according to their capacities are invited to share. But extremes must be avoided. Some educators err in confounding the person and the individual; others separate the two—"in order to grant personality the development and the freedom of expansion to which it aspires, they refuse all asceticism, they want man to yield fruit without being pruned. . . . In reality, what is especially important for the education and the progress of the human being, in the moral and spiritual order (as well as in the order of organic growth), is the interior principle, that is to say, nature and grace. The right educational means are but auxiliaries; the art, a co-operating art, at the service of this interior principle."[14] Man becomes what he ought to be, he becomes psychologically what he is metaphysically, namely a person, when the life of the spirit and of freedom dominates over that of passion and the senses.

It is apparent that Maritain's educational philosophy rests upon his conception of the human person and the distinction between person and individual, which critics have so often misunderstood. The nexus between his personalist philosophy and the democratic character of his educational ideals is also made plain. While he does not pretend to be a prophet, Maritain is convinced that unless we are overwhelmed by the nightmare of totalitarianism, the education of tomorrow will be animated by the democratic spirit. He envisions a personalist and humanist education for a personalist and democratic society. The watchword of *Education at the Crossroads* is "Integral Education for Integral Humanism."[15] The pluralist political philosophy he professes in *Man and the State* proclaims a democratic charter for education. He holds that the state and the educational system have a duty "to see to the teaching of that charter of common life, and thus to defend and promote the common good and the fundamental statute of the body politic even up to the common secular faith involved."

While the democratic state and the educational system it sustains cannot impose a philosophical or religious creed, and while the freedom of the person must be respected, every reasonable procedure ought to be employed to promote the democratic charter which is the core of the state's very existence. It would be absurd for teachers who believe in the values of democracy to be neutral about these values. Those who teach the democratic charter must believe in it with their whole hearts and stake their personal convictions upon it. The teachers would betray their mission, however, if they sought to make the school into either a stronghold of established society or an instrument for changing it. "It is neither for conservative nor for revolutionary purposes but for the general purpose of teaching them how to think, that they have to foster in the pupils the principles of the democratic charter."[16]

At this point we are confronted with the issue of education and tolerance in a pluralistic society. Maritain prefers to state the question in terms of truth and human fellowship, and it is a question of particular importance for democracies like our own, in which men and women coming from a great diversity of nationalities and religious or philosophical creeds must live together. If each of us were to attempt to impose his own beliefs upon his fellow-citizens, living together would become impossible. What then is genuine tolerance? It exists "when a man is firmly and absolutely convinced of a truth, or of what he holds to be a truth, and when he at the same time recognizes the right of those who deny this truth to exist, and to contradict him, and to speak their own mind, not because they are free from truth but because they seek truth in their own way, and because he respects in them human nature and human dignity and those very resources and living springs of the intellect and of conscience which make them potentially capable of attaining the truth he loves."[17]

THE REINTEGRATION OF THE HUMANITIES

The passages on the human person, culture, the democratic charter, and truth and tolerance which we have just presented afford ample evidence of the directive ideas behind Maritain's philosophy of education. His reflections upon the new social and cultural conditions that have emerged in the past few decades have convinced him that a thorough overhauling of our educational system must be undertaken. This does not mean the scuttling of liberal education. Far from it. Rather, liberal education must be extended to all, and in accordance with this extension the notion of what the humanities and the liberal arts involve must be rethought. The traditional list of the liberal arts needs recasting; the humanities should be envisaged from a more comprehensive viewpoint and their scattered members reassembled. In Chapter III, "Education and the Humanities," Maritain proposes a rather drastic revision of the classical and medieval "seven liberal arts," the Trivium and Quadrivium. His purpose in this is to provide for the vast development of knowledge in recent times and at the same time to preserve the liberal character of education. This revised curriculum deserves careful study and should be compared with other attempts to modernize the humanities.[18]

The Secretary of Health, Education and Welfare, Mr. Abraham Ribicoff, following C. P. Snow and other critics of contemporary education, has recently called attention to the unfortunate split in the intellectual life of our country and of the whole Western World: "Two great cultures—the sciences and the humanities—are growing up which scarcely know each other." We may well ask ourselves whether Catholic universities are as free as they should be from this division of the arts and sciences into two separate camps? Maritain's solution to the problem is far-reaching. On the level of universal knowledge, corresponding to that of collegiate or undergraduate education, the liberal arts must be reintegrated so as to comprehend, as they once did, the physical sciences, the human sciences, the literary disciplines, and philosophy. The physical sciences, and others patterned upon them, must regain their humanistic character. One of the principal contributions of Catholic education could, in our opinion, be the achievement of this synthesis of the humanities.

Physics and mathematics, according to Maritain, are liberal arts of the first rank and integral parts of the humanities. Indeed, physics is akin to poetry, if we look upon it in the light of the creative impulse within it which has led to so many marvelous discoveries. Maritain likes to imagine a curriculum in which all the humanities would be animated by the creative spirit. "In such a perspective," he says, "science and poetry are at one; humanity appears as a single being growing from generation to generation, thanks to the inner quickening spirit it has received from God."[19]

Perhaps the best way to restore the humanistic character of the physical sciences is through a study of the modes of scientific thought and of the history of scientific progress. The history of any discipline, far from being merely a collection of interesting facts *about* it and about the persons associated with it, affords matchless insight into the nature of that discipline and its mode of existence.[20] It would be in keeping with the best tradition of Catholic scholarship to emphasize the value of such historical studies, inasmuch as they enable us to see the organic connection between classical and medieval civilization and our own present-day culture.

LIBERAL EDUCATION FOR ALL

Over fifty years ago Nicholas Murray Butler pointed out that the task of education in a democracy is to develop among the whole people both intelligence and character.[21] Contemporary educators, Pragmatists and Marxists alike, agree on the thesis that all men in the measure of their capacities are entitled to equality of educational opportunity. This acknowledgment of a social phenomenon of immense historic significance attests to what Maritain calls a greater awareness of the dignity of the person and of the rights of the social person, particularly the worker.[22] These educators, however, do not agree on the meaning of universal education or on the kind of education it ought to be. The significance of Maritain's program lies in his insistence that everybody should in some measure receive *liberal* education.

Is this some sort of utopian illusion? In an age when specialists-in-training are expected to acquire increasingly intricate technical competence, how can anyone seek to impose upon the average man so overwhelming a burden as *universal* knowledge? Can we really expect, the skeptic will argue, all our young people of every degree of intellectual ability to benefit from liberal education? In his discussion of the French conception of the university, C. Bouglé asks, "Is it wise to open wide the sluices? Free education without selection means accepting every Tom, Dick, and Harry." The dull stand in the way of the gifted. The invitation to open the doors to everybody may involve cruel deceptions, like herding a mob into a cul-de-sac.[23]

Maritain is not, of course, proposing education without selection. In his judgment, we have been conceiving of liberal education in excessively or even exclusively intellectual terms. Intellectual activity is not the only one worthy of man; the Christian principle of the dignity of manual activity must be re-emphasized. Only in this way can the opposition between so-called popular education and liberal education be eliminated.[24] This will not be an easy thing to accomplish, and many compromises will and already are being made in American institutions of higher learning as they accept an increasingly higher percentage of high-school graduates annually. Maritain rejects any notion of compromise. He calls upon all, students and teachers, to put forth their best efforts, and enjoins upon them the pursuit of excellence.

In order to solve the problems involved in implementing the principle of liberal education for all, he draws what he himself regards as a distinction of far-reaching importance between natural intelligence and the intellectual virtues. In basic liberal education, the youth is not called upon to achieve the fully developed intellectual virtues which the mastery of a science or a discipline implies, any more than he is called upon to be a contemplative in either the full metaphysical or theological sense. Nevertheless, just as the contemplative depths of his mind should be awakened, so his desire to know the causes, the true explanation, of reality should be aroused.[25]

An educational philosophy which commits itself to the objective of liberal education for all must, according to Maritain, aim at universal knowledge attainable by a disciplined natural intelligence. What such a program requires of its students may well be as "stiff" as anything required of them by those who advocate a more highly rigorous scientific mode of presentation.[26] There is a certain ambiguity in the writings of some Catholic educators on this point. They maintain that the subjects should be taught scientifically even though the student ordinarily will not develop mature intellectual virtue until much later. Yet in practice they may be forced to settle for a good deal less than their teaching aims at. They may argue, for example, that metaphysics is the core of liberal education, yet admit that only a few students are able to grasp it.

The crucial issue here, however, is not whether either side is guilty of tolerating a lowering of standards but whether there is a significant difference in specific objectives. Even among Catholic educators, who are in basic accord on ultimate objectives, there are sharp differences of opinion on the immediate and proper aim of liberal education. As far as Maritain is concerned, his program neglects neither the dull nor the gifted student. By and large, and despite creditable efforts here and there, the gifted student has been neglected in American education. Students of talent would not be overlooked in Maritain's program since it is specifically ordered to developing the full measure of each person's ability. Such a program aims not merely at the refinement of one's powers of ratiocination but at the liberation of one's creative energies and intuitive powers.[27] Everybody is not expected to become a scientist, a sage, or a contemplative. Yet if the contemplative attitude were fostered in each individual from childhood, as is done in schools following the Montessori method, not only would each one find it easier to attain the comprehensive vision of reality—of God, man, and creation —on the level of universal knowledge, but those with the ability and the calling would advance more readily and surely in the acquisition of mature intellectual virtue in their later studies.

Maritain's ideal of liberal education for all has ramifications affecting both the higher and lower levels of education. This dynamic ideal runs like a leitmotiv through all of his writings on education. He looks upon it not only as "close to the requirements of natural law," but also as a "late fructification of Christian thought." Surely he is right in asserting that no educational philosophy should advocate such a goal more wholeheartedly than the Christian.[28]

Emmanuel Mounier, author of *The Personalist Manifesto*, once remarked, "*La femme aussi est une personne* (Woman, too, is a person)." Liberal education, then, should hold out equal opportunities for women. Maritain recognizes that American practical personalism, as we may call it, has in this as in many other matters been in the vanguard of true progress. "Youth is honored here," he remarks, "and youth is served, especially in the colleges, in a more liberal and generous way than in many other countries. Women here have a deep sense of their own mission with respect to culture. The teaching of young women hence appears as a thing doubly important and significant in the American way of life."[29] Maritain does not advocate an education for young men and women *identical* in all respects, as Chapter VII makes clear; his emphasis upon the development of the whole personality precludes such a misunderstanding.

In discussing the moral and spiritual values that education should inculcate (Chapter IV), Maritain pays tribute to American education for stressing the moral task incumbent upon the school. The paradox confronting the educator in this matter was never recognized more clearly than by Plato and Aristotle. As formulated by Maritain, the issue is: What is of greater importance than right moral conduct if young people are to become educated men and women? Yet is uprightness matter for teaching? You can teach what virtue is, its principles, its excellence, its obligatoriness, in moral philosophy and, in general, throughout the humanistic curriculum, but you cannot teach or impart virtue itself. Some ethicians speak of teaching virtue as though one could actually transmit a portion of one's virtue to the student; others speak more ambiguously of inculcating moral science, as though its acquisition involved the acquisition of the virtues as well. This thesis is rejected by Maritain with solid support from St. Thomas.[30]

If virtue cannot be taught, are we obliged then to say that the educational system should not be concerned at all with moral education? In Chapters IV and V, Maritain presents his solution to this vital question. "If the first responsibility of the school deals with the intellect and with knowledge," he says, "and if the first and direct responsibility for moral education belongs to the family group and the churches, nevertheless, the responsibility of the educational system in this respect is, however indirect, no less necessary."[31] It is the task of present-day education to develop a vision of the world in which convictions based on reason, about moral and spiritual values, are fostered. In an age when men are confronted with relativistic moral theories, this task of the school has become more urgent than ever before.

THE DISTINCTIVE FEATURES
OF CHRISTIAN EDUCATION

It cannot be emphasized too strongly that in his educational philosophy Maritain is not merely attempting to provide a blueprint for the Catholic college but is seeking to explain the principles governing all liberal education in a free and pluralistic society. These principles should be those of a personalist and humanist philosophy of education and of culture. Yet his view on the teaching of theology is unmistakably clear, and he quotes Cardinal Newman in its support.[32] He would also make his own the inspiring words of Pope Pius XI:

The proper and immediate end of Christian education is to co-operate with divine grace in forming the true and perfect Christian, that is, to form Christ Himself in those regenerated by baptism. . . . For precisely this reason, Christian education takes in the whole aggregate of human life, physical and spiritual, intellectual and moral, individual, domestic and social, *not with a view of reducing it in any way,* but in order to elevate, regulate and perfect it, in accordance with the example and teaching of Christ.[33]

In Chapter VI, "Some Typical Aspects of Christian Education," Maritain develops more fully than anywhere else the distinctively Christian features of his educational ideal. Some of the ideas expressed in this essay are proper to a Christian philosophy of education. Others go beyond the scope of philosophy, as, for example, his recommendations regarding the fostering of liturgical knowledge and liturgical life in Catholic students. The Christian philosophy of education is neither the equivalent of nor a substitute for a Christian theology of education. It is enriched by insights deriving from Christian wisdom yet remains truly philosophical. It is based upon Christian anthropology, especially the metaphysics of the human person and the philosophical doctrine of man's nature as a substantial unity of soul and body. It is subordinated to Christian moral philosophy, from which it derives its views concerning the end of man and the role of virtue in human life. It is related to the philosophy of culture or civilization which extends to all phases of human life. It is supported by social and political philosophy, and in concert with it promotes the true emancipation of the person.

Every Catholic educator would hold that there is a Christian philosophy of education, in the sense of a reasoned presentation of Catholic thought about God, man, and the universe, and about the goals of education for a creature considered in the supernatural as well as the natural aspect of his being.[34] However, not all would agree with Maritain's notion of Christian philosophy in the strict sense of the term, and therefore not all would accept his notion of a Christian philosophy of education in this sense. Yet many would accept certain of his proposals for the reform of education.

The Christian philosophy of education views the intellectual and moral education of man in the light of his nature and end in a strictly philosophical way, yet with the aid of the light shed upon these matters by theology. The theologian follows what might be termed the divine order, proceeding from God to creatures; the philosopher follows the human order, proceeding from creatures to their Maker.[35] Fortified and illumined by theology, Christian philosophy differs from it in its principles, methods of exposition and of demonstration, and in its formal object. The Christian philosophy of education, likewise, enters into dialogue or controversy, as the case may be, with other philosophies of education in a strictly rational manner, but its *perspective* is different, and it would be disingenuous to conceal this fact.[36]

The question as to whether or not there is a Christian philosophy in the strict sense has been the subject of lively and periodically renewed debate among Catholic philosophers for over thirty years. A concrete example of what Maritain means by Christian philosophy is to be found in "The Conquest of Freedom." This essay is a genuinely philosophical explanation of terminal freedom as freedom of exultation, and of man's self-fulfillment in attaining it, yet it has benefited greatly from the stimulus afforded by contact with Christian theology.[37]

The doctrine of the conquest of freedom is at the heart of Maritain's educational theory, although this essay itself is not concerned with education as such. We have included it in the present volume because without it one fails to seize the deeper significance of Maritain's philosophy of education.

Maritain has touched upon the primacy of inner freedom in many of his works, as, for example, in *Some Reflections on Culture and Liberty.* In *Education at the Crossroads,* he states that "the prime goal of education is the conquest of internal and spiritual liberty, to be achieved by the individual person, or, in other words, his liberation through knowl-

edge and wisdom, good will, and love. . . . This conquest
of being, this progressive attainment of new truths . . . opens
and enlarges our mind and life, and really situates them in
freedom and autonomy."[38] In *The Rights of Man and the
Natural Law,* Maritain shows incisively the connection between the conquest of freedom and the more profound awareness, the *prise de conscience,* of the dignity of the human
person which has been achieved in our time.[39] In Chapter
VII, speaking of democratic education, he says that it is one
"which helps human persons to shape themselves . . . discipline themselves, to love and to praise the high truths
which are the very root and safeguard of their dignity, to
respect in themselves and in others human nature and conscience, and to conquer themselves in order to win their
liberty."[40]

The doctrine developed in "The Conquest of Freedom" is
bipolar. The metaphysics of the person (with its distinction
between person and individual) constitutes the vertical pole;
its horizontal pole extends to true political and social emancipation. This doctrine provides the basis for a philosophy of
culture, and holds up an ideal of true freedom and true personality which education should look upon as its objective.[41]

The intimate relationship between liberty and education
is treated by Maritain in *"Le Problème de l'École Publique
en France."*[42] There are two moments of liberty, he tells us—
that of the child's first mysterious choice between good and
evil, and that of the adolescent's decision to accept or reject
on mature, or presumably mature, grounds the beliefs he
has accepted from childhood. Evidently, the latter moment
is crucial to the philosophy of education. The importance of
recognizing and respecting this liberty of young men and
women is brought out by the learned Benedictine, Dom
Aelred Graham. "Intellectual maturity can never be achieved
where there has been no free play of the mind. And where
the mind has free play, there will come the inevitable challenge to received opinions. Consequently it is to be expected

that a boy at college will have difficulties about religion. If he has not, then I would suggest either that he is exceptionally dull-witted or that there is something wrong with the college. . . . What is required, I submit, is not that a boy should evade the challenge by taking refuge either in servile obedience or in blank scepticism, but that he should re-integrate his religious thinking at the adult level. And to do this he normally needs to be helped."[43]

Maritain points out that in Christian education, philosophy and theology should be the keystone of the "edifice of learning of the Christian college ordered to wisdom." He suggests that religious training can be integrated on the collegiate level through its vital connections with theology and philosophy, as well as through the fostering of liturgical life and a love of Sacred Scripture.[44]

The Christian school, according to Maritain, must deal with the whole of human culture; its students should be taught to respect the values of Eastern civilizations as well as those of the Western World. It is the light in which ideas and values are viewed that makes our approach Christian. Our watchword must be "enlargement," he says, "Christian-inspired enlargement, not narrowing, even Christian-centered narrowing, of the humanities."[45]

Maritain would welcome the aid of any of the approaches or techniques of modern society—e.g. educational television —that would promote such an enlargement. Yet in an age dominated by mass production, conformism, mass communication, and mass culture, he would encourage individuals and small groups in the promoting of a Christian-inspired enlargement of education. In keeping with his personalist philosophy, Maritain would urge the formation of self-organized teams of students. He recommends, too, the breaking down of rigid departmental and divisional barriers in our universities, the creation of schools of "orientated humanities," of institutes of advanced research, and of "schools in spiritual life"—houses of hospitality for the renewal of the spirit.[46]

Always the emphasis is upon whatever will facilitate greater communion, freedom, and communication between persons.

The notion of play enjoys a central role in Maritain's proposals for the liberal education of the future, in which popular education is to become liberal and liberal education popular. This is no mere slogan. Going beyond what he says about play in *Education at the Crossroads*, Maritain broadens its scope so as to include the notion of informal and unsystematic learning. In the schools of the "intellectual-service training center" the humanities are matters of formal learning while craftsmanship and various kinds of manual activity are matters of informal learning or play. In the "manual-service training center" the procedure is reversed. His answer, then, to the repeated charge that the masses could not profit from liberal education is that "in the schools of the manual-service training center education in all matters pertaining to the humanities and liberal arts would be surprisingly successful if it were given not by way of formal teaching but by way of play and informal learning."[47] In this conception of play as free expansion of the spirit, as a rejoicing in activities one is not *obliged* to perform, Maritain contributes yet another idea of extraordinary value for future education.

Maritain is fully aware of the fact that certain of his proposals are considered impracticable, and that a long time may elapse before attempts are made to put them into execution. He realizes that what he is proposing, though in accord with the deeper movement of history, may be in conflict with superficial currents of thought. He has given us a personalist and humanist philosophy of education which is not only for today but for tomorrow. Despite the pragmatism besetting American education, it is, he believes, a profoundly human and personalist venture, and he is confident that in the pluralistic society from which it springs, the principles of Christian educational philosophy will take root and flourish.

MARITAIN AS PHILOSOPHER OF EDUCATION

In this Introduction we have not sought to evaluate the specific features of Maritain's educational program but, rather, to capture the spirit of his philosophy of education. Throughout the ages the wise men—the humanists, philosophers, and theologians—have had their say about the education of man. Education is at once a speculative question of the first order and a practical question of the utmost urgency. It involves a philosopher's deepest convictions about man, but it also demands action, for the young continue to invade the portals of our schools and colleges, and educated in some fashion they must be. Many are the thinkers who have enriched our understanding of the theoretical and practical aspects of education; the roster of their distinguished names is too lengthy even to be listed here. The Syntopicon of the Great Books of the Western World lists a multitude of them from Homer to Freud, from Plutarch to Hook and Conant.

The thought of Jacques Maritain on education might profitably be compared with that of the classical authors, with fellow Catholic educators, and with other contemporary philosophers. Yet he cannot be compared strictly with most of these because his perspective is different, being that of the Christian philosophy of education. Maritain has much in common with the sages of the ancient and medieval periods—with Plato and Aristotle on man's rational nature and the dignity of contemplation, with Augustine and Aquinas on the end of man and the primacy of love-in-contemplation. Yet his is a twentieth-century philosophy of education and not a mere recapitulation of classic ideas and ideals. Maritain shares the concerns of contemporary philosophers like Dewey and Whitehead on the educational needs of man in a democratic and pluralistic society, yet his first prin-

ciples and ultimate objectives differ from theirs. The medieval thinkers, although able to teach us much about
philosophy, made no attempt to elaborate a philosophy of
education as such. The educational doctrine of Augustine in
On Christian Doctrine and of Hugh of St. Victor in *Didas-
calicon* is, for all the philosophy and humanistic knowledge
it contains, a Christian theology of education.

The aim of Jacques Maritain is to provide an educational
philosophy which, although indebted to the Greek and Ro-
man tradition, and steadied and enlightened by Christian
theology, is suited to the needs of contemporary man and is
characterized by specifically philosophical principles and
methods. His philosophy of education is distinctively Christian because it incorporates insights which are "fructifica-
tions of Christian thought," such as liberal education for all,
the primacy of the contemplative spirit, the conquest of
freedom, and the dignity of manual work. It is distinctively
philosophical because it fully recognizes the implications of
man's existence in diverse spheres—the intellectual and
moral, the individual and social—and sets forth an educational program for the full development of the human being
both as a person and as a participant in society. This Christian philosophy of education proclaims for all men, in the
measure of their receptivity and responsiveness, the fulfillment of their being by the liberation of the power of contemplation and of latent creative energies.[48]

A spirit of freedom and creativity, a spirit of contemplation permeate Maritain's ideal "educational republic." Yet
the personalism of this philosopher is not utopian. It is practical in its specific recommendations for the school of today,
and in its prognostications for the school of tomorrow. And
it is practical in its insistence that the school must care for
each one of its charges. As Maritain says, the teacher must
revere the mysterious identity of each of his pupils. Maritain
and Newman are of one mind here, although their particular
conceptions of the university may differ. A university is,

Newman tells us, "an Alma Mater, knowing her children one by one, not a foundry or a mint or a treadmill."[49]

The studies in this volume, together with *Education at the Crossroads*, comprise the principal writings by Jacques Maritain on the subject of education. The sources from which they have been taken are indicated in the bibliography, which also contains references to other writings by and about Maritain. Several of these studies were written originally as lectures or prepared for special occasions. There was, consequently, some unavoidable repetition in the treatment of the basic themes. As editors we have attempted to correct this by revising and condensing the material where necessary. For example, in Chapter III, which was previously unpublished, we have eliminated certain passages which were duplicated in the other chapters. This revision has been done with the approval of Prof. Maritain himself and with the utmost care to preserve his own text with a minimum of alteration. It has been our intention to order the studies in such a way that this book would not merely be a collection of essays on education but would manifest the synthesis of cultural, social, and metaphysical insights embodied in Maritain's Christian philosophy of education.

Donald and Idella Gallagher

NOTES TO INTRODUCTION

1. Vd. Tad Guzie, S.J., *The Analogy of Learning: An Essay Toward a Thomistic Psychology of Learning*, with a preface by R. J. Henle, S.J. (New York: Sheed and Ward, 1960), pp. 11–17. The Introduction comprises a bibliographical survey from 1900 to the present of all Thomistic literature concerned with educational and learning theory. The author mentions many fields of study in this area awaiting adequate investigation by Thomists. "Too much has been presumed for too long." According to Guzie, Maritain is one of the few whose work contains a sound psychological interpretation of the way we actually learn, yet he introduces ideas difficult to interpret, such as that of the preconscious of the intellect (pp. 9–10).

2. See p. 69 below.

3. Vd. the address of the same title by E. J. Drummond, S.J. (Milwaukee: Marquette University Press, 1955), and also Gerard Smith, S.J., *The Truth That Frees* (Milwaukee: Marquette University Press, 1956; an Aquinas Lecture).

4. Chapter II, p. 48.

5. Vd. George R. Geiger, "An Experimentalist Approach to Education," Robert S. Cohen, "On the Marxist Philosophy of Education," in *Modern Philosophies and Education*, the Fifty-Fourth Yearbook of the National Society for the Study of Education, Part I (Chicago: University of Chicago Press, 1955).

6. Quoted in *Great Issues in Education* (Chicago: The Great Books Foundation, 1956), Volume II. Cf. Dewey's remark in *Democracy and Education:* "If we are willing to conceive education as the process of forming fundamental dispositions, intellectual and emotional, toward nature and fellow men, philosophy may even be defined *as the general theory*

of education", (*Intelligence in the Modern World: John Dewey's Philosophy*, edited by Joseph Ratner; New York: The Modern Library, 1939, p. 259). Cf. "John Dewey in Context," by Beatrice Zedler, in *Some Philosophers on Education*, edited by Donald A. Gallagher (Milwaukee: Marquette University Press, 1956), pp. 1–25.

7. Vd. Francis C. Wade, S.J., "Saint Thomas Aquinas and Teaching," in *Some Philosophers on Education*, pp. 67–85. This study, as Guzie notes (*op. cit.*, p. 10), explicitly considers the unity of man as a basis for learning theory.

8. Cf. Geiger and Cohen in the studies cited in Note 5 above. We do not mean to imply that Marxism, a dogmatic philosophy, and pragmatism, a relativistic one, are alike, but there are some curious parallels in their respective outlooks.

9. Chapter III, pp. 86–90.

10. Vd. Alfred North Whitehead, *The Aims of Education* (New York: The New American Library, a Mentor Book), 1949.

11. Chapter II, p. 82.

12. *The Commonweal*, XLIV, April 26, 1946, p. 36. See Bibliography for reference to this series of articles, based on *Education at the Crossroads*. For text from which this passage is quoted see Appendix A.

13. Jacques Maritain, "Religion and Culture," *Essays in Order* (New York: The Macmillan Company, 1931), p. 8.

14. Jacques Maritain, "The Human Person and Society," *Scholasticism and Politics* (Garden City, N.Y.: Image Books, Doubleday & Co., 1960), pp. 69–70. For text from which this quotation is made see Appendix B. Cf. Jacques Maritain, *The Person and the Common Good* (New York: Charles Scribner's Sons, 1947), pp. 35–36.

15. *Op. cit.*, p. 88. See Bibliography for complete reference.

16. Chapter II, p. 59. See "Education and the Democratic Charter," in *Man and the State* (Chicago: University of Chicago Press, 1951), pp. 119–126. Cf. Chapter II of this volume, pp. 62–68.

17. Jacques Maritain, *Truth and Human Fellowship* (Princeton: Princeton University Press, 1957), pp. 4 and 11. This essay is reprinted in *On the Use of Philosophy*, by Jacques Maritain (Princeton: Princeton University Press, 1961).

18. Vd. Chapter III, pp. 91–93. This liberal arts program should be compared with that proposed in *Education at the Cross-roads*, Chapter III. For two extremely informative studies on the liberal arts, see Pierre Conway, O.P. and Benedict Ashley, O.P., *The Liberal Arts in St. Thomas Aquinas*, a Thomist Reprint (Washington: The Thomist Press, 1959), 75 pp., and also Fr. Ashley's *Arts of Learning and Communication* (Dubuque, Iowa: Priory Press, 1958). Among other studies, the reader should consult James V. Mullaney, "The Liberal Arts in the Aristotelian-Thomist Scheme of Knowledge," *The Thomist*, XIX (1956), pp. 481–505; *The St. John's Program, A Report* (Annapolis: St. John's College Press, 1955); *The Liberal Education of the Christian Person* (Chicago: St. Xavier College, 1953).

19. Chapter IV, p. 107.

20. Professor Geiger (*art. cit.*, p. 306; see Note 5 above) stresses the humanistic character of the sciences from the experimentalist point of view.

21. *True and False Democracy* (New York: The Macmillan Company, 1907), pp. 100–101. Dr. Butler (1862–1947), philosopher and educator, was President of Columbia University from 1901 to 1945.

22. *The Rights of Man and the Natural Law* (New York: Charles Scribner's Sons, 1945), pp. 92–93.

23. "The French Conception of the University," *The University in a Changing World*, edited by W. Kotschnig and E. Prys (Oxford University Press; London: Humphrey Milford, 1932), pp. 48–49. (See in the same symposium the fine essay of Dietrich von Hildebrand, "The Conception of a Catholic University," pp. 197–224).

24. Chapter VI, pp. 149–150.

25. Vd. *Education at the Crossroads*, pp. 40–44 and 62–63.

26. The different points of view to which we refer are illustrated in the perennial discussions about the proper order and procedure in the teaching of the philosophy course. For Maritain's view, see Chapter VI, pp. 139–140.

27. Chapter VI, pp. 150–153.

28. *Ibid.*, pp. 147–148.

29. Chapter VII, pp. 155–156.

30. Jacques Maritain, "The Philosophy of Faith" and "Reflections on Moral Philosophy" in *Science and Wisdom* (New York: Charles Scribner's Sons, 1940).
31. Chapter IV, p. 105.
32. Chapter II, p. 79.
33. Pius XI, "Christian Education of Youth," *Five Great Encyclicals*, ed. Gerald Treacy, S.J. (New York: The Paulist Press, 1945), pp. 64–65.
34. Cf. William J. McGucken, S.J., *The Philosophy of Catholic Education* (New York: The America Press, 1943), a pamphlet reprinted from *Philosophies of Education*, the Forty-First Yearbook of the National Society for the Study of Education. Dr. Vincent E. Smith, in *The School Examined: Its Aim and Content* (Milwaukee: The Bruce Publishing Company, 1960), p. viii, states that there is, in the proper sense of the term, no Catholic philosophy of education. There is a Catholic theology of education. He proceeds to develop a comprehensive program of education for the Catholic college, based upon the fivefold scheme, Logic, Mathematics, Natural Science, Moral Science, Metaphysics, crowned by Sacred Doctrine.
35. Saint Thomas Aquinas, *On the Truth of the Catholic Faith Summa Contra Gentiles*, Book Two: Creation, translated by James F. Anderson (Garden City, N.Y.: Image Books, Doubleday & Co., 1955), Chapter IV, pp. 34–35.
36. Maritain remarks that even in the subjects which are not influenced by theology, as philosophy is—e.g., mathematics (there is no Christian mathematics)—the influence of the Christian teacher will make itself felt (Chapter VI, pp. 136–137). Father Leo R. Ward quotes a letter from Maritain (*New Life in Catholic Schools*, Saint Louis: B. Herder Book Company, 1958, pp. 94–95), in which the latter says, "Necessary as competence in his particular field may be, a Catholic intellectual is not a scientist or a teacher or an artist *plus* a Christian. His inner spiritual life *superabounds spontaneously* in the very *mode* of his activity, if his life is deep enough. No 'proselytism' here, therefore. The very way in which he performs his ordinary tasks may convey some superior inspiration without his being even aware of it."

37. Vd. the text from the *Summa Contra Gentiles* quoted in Chapter VIII, pp. 177–178. This passage, a commentary on St. Paul, Maritain looks upon as one of the "great texts absolutely fundamental for the spiritual constitution of humanity."

38. *Op. cit.*, pp. 11–12.

39. *Op. cit.*, pp. 110–111. "The impulses which emanate from the Bible," remarks Karl Jaspers, "work even where no one is aware of their origin." (*Nietzsche and Christianity*, Chicago: Henry Regnery, 1961, p. viii).

40. Chapter VII, p. 158.

41. There is reciprocal action among these philosophies and in the real movements they seek to explain. The historical movement toward emancipation leads to a recognition of the rights of the person, including the workingman, and this recognition leads to a demand for greater emancipation.

42. See Bibliography II, for complete reference to this study.

43. "Towards a Catholic Concept of Education in a Democracy," *Harvard Educational Review*, XXXI (Fall, 1961), p. 404.

44. Chapter VI, pp. 140–143.

45. *Ibid.*, p. 136.

46. *Education at the Crossroads*, p. 84; cf. the profound remarks on the "centers of spiritual life" in *The Range of Reason* (New York: Charles Scribner's Sons, 1951), p. 49.

47. Chapter VI, p. 153.

48. Maria Letizia Cassata pays this tribute to Maritain in *La Pedagogia di Jacques Maritain* (Palermo: Boccone del Povero, 1953, p. 98): "La viva attualità con cui egli ha avvertito il problema educativo, come la forza di liberazione della persona, gli ha dato una visione chiara e completa della formazione interiore, che deve seguire l'uomo per farsi personalità. Il suo ideale pedagogico quindi è la formazione di una coscienza morale vera, è la formazione dell'uomo secondo l'immagine di Dio."

49. John Henry Newman, *The Idea of a University* (Garden City, New York: Image Books, 1959), p. 165.

THE
EDUCATION
OF MAN

Chapter One

PHILOSOPHY AND EDUCATION

The universal human value of Catholic education is demonstrated in contrast to the various partial and one-sided systems devised by modern writers. Nowadays, when the naturalistic and socialistic theories of education are beginning here and there to sanction the most radical experiments, and when we see developing in many countries a powerful effort to train, by a method adapted to youth, a new man of a completely atheistic type, it is necessary that Catholics should understand the importance of the problems presented by modern education and prepare to maintain the traditional methods on a level with all the real progress that the newer education has been able to register.

Every theory of education is based on a conception of life and, consequently, is associated necessarily with a system of philosophy. Without going back to the great thinkers of the past, we are aware of the fact that in our own day Naturalistic Philosophy has given rise to a naturalistic education (Spencer); Socialism to a social education (Durkheim, Dewey, Natorp, Kerschensteiner); Nationalism to a national and state system of education (Fichte and the Prussian School System). Education "follows the flux and reflux of philosophical currents." It is not an autonomous science, but dependent upon Philosophy. This is an elementary truth that is beginning to be quite generally recognized today, particularly in Germany.

Thinking men are beginning to realize that certain theories which were largely in vogue during the nineteenth century were in reality but narrow prejudices lacking in objective value. There was, for example, a prejudice in favor of a scientific psychology, in the positivistic meaning of the phrase. It was maintained that natural science was the only science, to the exclusion of metaphysics. Yet when a science has man for its object, it comes into the category of the sciences of values. To eliminate personality with its system of values is to deny the very nature of these departments of knowledge and of life. Then there was a prejudice in favor of basing education exclusively on psychology. To be sure, psychology is one of the fundamental bases of education; yet the knowledge of that subject is but one presupposition of the science of education. It is clear that the teacher must adapt himself to the child, but education properly so called does not begin until the child adapts himself to the teacher and to the culture, the truths and the systems of value which it is the mission of the teacher to transmit to the child. If Psychologism, now generally abandoned, still influences the field of pedagogy, it is to the greatest detriment of sound notions of education. Another prejudice was in favor of basing education solely on practical experience. With regard to this, we may say that, while practical experience is indispensable, it is unintelligible except in the light of the principles that direct it. Still another theory maintained that education should be restricted to educational methodology alone, to that which is the material of education exclusively. Methods, programs, organization, educational technique are, without doubt, important; but they are, after all, merely secondary. First must come the truth to which the teacher should bear witness. In other words, we must first define the ideal of life that is to serve as a guide in the training of the intellect and the development of personality.

Education is by nature a function of philosophy, of metaphysics. Every educator worships a deity—for Spencer it is Nature; for Comte, Humanity; for Rousseau, Liberty; for Freud, Sex; for Durkheim and Dewey, Society; for Wundt, Culture; for Emerson, the Individual. Or perhaps everything is reduced to a question of adaptation to the child or of letting nature take its course, which is tantamount to denying education. In truth, if the modern world is so concerned with education, it is not because of the fact that it has made any extraordinary discoveries in that field; it is, as Chesterton says, because modern man has lost his bearings; he knows neither where he is nor where he is going. Without doubt, this is why he is so concerned about others.

As a matter of fact, "the great battles of education are being waged today beyond the frontiers of education properly so called; in other words, in the domain of philosophy." Rightly speaking, the term "educational philosophy" should be substituted for "educational psychology" or "education." And because, in the practical order, ends play the role of principles, it is only by thus attaching and subordinating itself to philosophy that education will be able to acquire that real scientific character, a mocking counterfeit of which Positivism pretends to offer.

The *Philosophia Perennis* has for its object to re-establish the real hierarchy of things, both human and divine, and to restore to spiritual and metaphysical values the priority that rightly belongs to them. And yet, properly speaking, it is not merely a question of metaphysical values that concerns us here. If the conception of man, of human life, human culture, and human destiny is the basis of all education, we must insist that there is no really complete science of education, just as there is no really complete political science, except such as is correlated with and subordinate to the science of theology. The reason is simple. Man is not merely a natural being, an *ens naturale*, but is called to a supernatural end. He is in a state either of fallen nature or of nature restored. The existence or non-existence of original sin and the effects thereof, the *vulnera naturae*, is a question of no small importance to education. As a practical science dealing with the complete formation of man, it is a theological discipline. And so, if the family has the obligation of continuing through the process of education *quasi in utero spirituali*, as St. Thomas says, the work of generation; and if civil society, the aim of which is to promote the practice of virtue in the social body, has the right and the duty of regulating educational matters in the interest of the common welfare and in conformity with the natural and divine law; then the Church of Christ, by reason of her spiritual and supernatural relation to mankind, must be acknowledged as the Educator *par excellence* of the children of man.

What theory can give to all this wealth of material the intellectual form it needs if not that synthetic doctrine which comprehends all reality, which is in conformity with the principles of reason and the facts of experience, and of which St. Thomas Aquinas is the great Master? Thomistic Philosophy holds a veritable treasure of cultural values which, it would seem, it is our duty to unlock to the expectant world.

An educational theory systematically built upon the principles of St. Thomas and drawing its inspiration from his store of wisdom will be able to give real scientific consistency to Catholic thought and practice in the field of education. Only such a theory will be able to unify the many divergent points of view and settle the many difficult questions which up to the present have too often been stated without being defined. This is the case, for example, with the question of the relations between the individual and society. The conflict between these, real as it undoubtedly is, need not be essential if it be true that man is a social as well as rational animal and that society as such exists for the attainment of human and moral ends. St. Thomas, as we have attempted to show elsewhere, is the only thinker who has formulated a perfectly correct idea of human nature, which is the central factor in education. His is the only theory that draws a clear distinction between the natural and the supernatural order while pointing out their essential accord. It is the only theory that establishes the primacy of intellect in the order of substances and of speculative knowledge. It is the only theory that maintains the primacy of will, of love, in the practical order; that is, in the field of human acts, in the formation of character, and in the conduct of life. In brief, it is to St. Thomas we must go for enlightenment with regard to the factors without a complete understanding of which a sound theory of education is impossible.

Educators, however, must not expect too much from education. A famous educator once declared in the hearing of this writer that "we must defend the catechism against education." St. Thomas holds that the teacher actually engenders knowledge in the soul of the pupil, and this is equally true of moral habits and of virtue; but, in so doing, he acts as an instrumental and not as an efficient cause. His duty is not to mold the child's mind arbitrarily as the potter molds the lifeless clay; rather it is his task to assist the mind, the living, spiritual being, which he is endeavoring to develop, and which in that process of development must be the principal agent. For education, like life, is, in the words of philosophy, an immanent activity. In like manner, the teacher's task is to co-operate with God, Who is the Source of Truth and the First Cause, Whose action surpasses that of all created agencies, Who can obtain results that no human teacher can obtain, and Who is continually teaching His rational creatures by various means, at one time using force, at another, persuasion; now employing external agencies and now speaking directly to the individual soul. "The wisdom of Providence," says St. Augustine, "guards us from without and instructs us from within."

Chapter Two

THOMIST VIEWS ON EDUCATION

BASIC ORIENTATION

It is advisable, I think, to draw a clear distinction between the basic philosophical issues on which theories of education depend and the questions of a more practical nature which bear on concrete application and the technique of education. So I shall, as a rule, divide into two parts the considerations that I should like to submit, one dealing with philosophical principles, the other with practical application.

In a general way, I would say that the Thomist outlook is in opposition to the philosophical systems (notably pragmatism) to which progressive education most often appeals for support, but agrees in many respects with the practical ways and methods of progressive education when they are not led astray by prejudice or ideological intemperance, and decidedly favors their concern with the inner resources and vital spontaneity of the pupil. In many cases, and from a practical point of view, the conflicts between different schools of thought seem to me to relate less to absolutely incompatible views than to the relative emphasis which is to be put on various complementary aspects. In educational matters, as in all matters dealing with man's life, what is of chief importance is the direction of the process, and the implied hierarchy of values.

Concerning Philosophical Principles. Underlying all questions concerning the basic orientation of education, there is the *philosophy of knowledge* to which the educator consciously or unconsciously subscribes. It is regrettable that more often than not this philosophy of knowledge, in our current practice, is accepted ready-made rather than critically examined.

Thomist philosophy maintains that there is a difference in nature between the senses (where knowledge depends on material action exercised upon bodily organs, and which attain things in their actual and singular existence but only as enigmatically manifested by the diversified physical energies they display) and the intellect (which is spiritual in essence and attains, through the universal concepts it brings out from sense experience, the constitutive features of what things are).

This basic point is denied by empiricism. According to empiricist philosophy there is no distinction of nature, but only of degree, between the senses and the intellect. As a result, human knowledge is simply sense-knowledge (that is, animal knowledge) more evolved and elaborated than in other mammals. And not only is human knowledge entirely encompassed in, and limited to, sense-experience (a point which Kant, while reacting against Hume, admitted like Hume) but, to produce its achievements in the sphere of sense-experience, human knowledge uses no other specific forces and means than the forces and means that are at play in sense-knowledge.

Thus, from the Thomist point of view, the empiricist theory of knowledge is of a nature inevitably to warp, in the long run, the educational endeavor. And this happens in a rather insidious way: For if it is true, in actual fact, that reason differs specifically from the senses, then the paradox with which we are confronted is that empiricism, in actual fact, uses reason while denying the specific power of reason, on the basis of a theory which reduces reason's knowledge and life, which are characteristic of man, to sense-knowledge and life, which are characteristic of animals. Hence, there are confusions and inconsistencies which will inevitably reflect on the educational work. Not only does the empiricist think as a man and use reason, a power superior in nature to the senses, while at the same time he is denying this very specificity of reason, but what he speaks of and describes as sense-knowledge is not exactly sense-knowledge, but sense-knowledge *plus* unconsciously introduced intellective ingredients; that is, the empiricist discusses sense-knowledge in which he has made room for reason without recognizing it. This confusion comes about all the more easily as, on the one hand, the senses are, in actual existence, more or less permeated with reason in man, and, on the other, the merely sensory psychology of animals, especially of the higher vertebrates, goes very far in its own realm and imitates intellectual knowledge to a considerable extent. It is thus possible to go a long way in educating a child of man as if he were a child of some simian particularly evolved and supposedly civilized. An educational theory based on empiricism will cover the whole development of the youth and be interested in the cultivation of the rational and spiritual powers of his mind, but in doing so it will be ignorant of the very nature of these powers, disregard their proper needs and aspirations, and bring everything back to the ambiguous level of the development of a child of man in terms of simple animal life and development.

Let us go a step further. In the eyes of Thomist philosophy any merely instrumentalist theory of knowledge is open to similar objections—by reason of the empiricist presuppositions on which any merely instrumentalist philosophy of knowledge rests. It is an unfortunate mistake to define human thought as an organ of response to the stimuli and situations of the environment, that is to say, to define it in terms of animal knowledge and reaction, for such a definition exactly corresponds to the way of "thinking" peculiar to animals without reason. The truth of the matter is just the opposite. It is because human ideas attain being, or what things *are* (even if they do so in the most indirect manner, and in the symbols of physico-mathematical science); it is because human thought is a vital energy of spiritual intuition grasping things in their intelligible consistency and universal values; it is because thinking begins, not with difficulties, but with *insights*, and ends in insights whose truth is established by rational demonstration or experimental verification, not by pragmatic sanction, that human thought is able to illumine experience and to dominate, control, and refashion the world. At the beginning of human action, insofar as it is human, there is truth, grasped or believed to be grasped, for the sake of truth. Without trust in truth, there is no human effectiveness.

Thus, for Thomist philosophy, knowledge is a value in itself and an end in itself; and truth consists in the conformity of the mind with reality—with what is or exists independently of the mind. The intellect tends to grasp and conquer being. Its aim and its joy are essentially disinterested. And "perfect" or "grown-up" knowledge ("science" in the broad Aristotelian sense) reaches certainties which are valid in their pure objectivity—whatever the bents and interests of the individual or collective man may be—and are unshakably established through the intuition of first principles and the logical necessity of the deductive or inductive process. Thus, that superior kind of knowledge which is wisdom, because it deals not only with mastering natural phenomena but with penetrating the primary and most universal *raisons d'être* and with enjoying, as a final fruition, the spiritual delight of truth and the sapidity of being, fulfills the supreme aspiration of the intellectual nature and its thirst for liberation.

There is no other foundation for the educational task than

the eternal saying "It is truth which sets man free." It appears, by the same token, that education is fully human education only when it is liberal education, preparing the youth to exercise his power to think in a genuinely free and liberating manner—that is to say, when it equips him for truth and makes him capable of judging according to the worth of evidence, of enjoying truth and beauty for their own sake, and of advancing, when he has become a man, toward wisdom and some understanding of those things which bring to him intimations of immortality.

Concerning Practical Application. I have just spoken of the stage where intellectual virtues have come to completion and of knowledge as science. This led us far beyond the scope of school and college education. It must be pointed out, in particular, that, precisely because scientific knowledge is "perfect" or "grown-up" knowledge, it is fitted to adults, not to children—to those who know, not to those who are in the process of acquiring knowledge. As to the techniques of education, Thomist philosophy, which insists that man is body as well as spirit and that nothing comes into the intellect if not through the senses, heartily approves of the general emphasis put by progressive education on the essential part to be played in the process by the senses and the hands and by the natural interests of the child. It also emphasizes sense-training (both as to perception and memory) and the direct experiential approach—but on the condition that all this should be directed toward the awakening of the intellectual powers and the development of the sense of truth.

A crucial point should be emphasized in this connection.[1] We have to understand the far-reaching significance and the practical import of the distinction between *natural intelligence* and the *habitus* or ἕξεις which Aristotle and

[1] Another point would deal with the typical "worlds of knowledge" which are peculiar to the main stages of the educational process. Cf. my book *Education at the Crossroads*, pp. 60–62.

Thomas Aquinas called *intellectual virtues*. Art (each of the specifically distinct arts), science (each of the specifically distinct sciences), and wisdom are intellectual virtues. Really to know a science is to possess the intellectual virtue which constitutes this science in the soul. And the intellectual virtues are special energies which grow in intelligence through exercise in a given object, as superadded perfections, superior in quality to the capacity of what I call *natural intelligence;* that is to say, of intelligence considered in its bare nature. Thus we have two quite different states for intelligence: *natural intelligence* and *intelligence as scientifically formed and equipped,* or, in Thomist language, *intelligence perfected by the intellectual virtues.*

My contention is that education, especially liberal education, has essentially to cultivate and liberate, form and equip intelligence, and to prepare for the development of the intellectual virtues, but that this development itself, once the threshold of virtue has been crossed, is necessarily particularized to a given branch of knowledge. So no *universal knowledge* is possible at the level of intellectual virtues or at the level of science (except that kind of universal knowledge which knows things only in their fundamentals and which is proper to wisdom, the supreme intellectual virtue). But a kind of *universal knowledge* is possible at the level of *natural intelligence* or at a level which is neither scientific nor philosophical. At this level of natural intelligence, the youth can be offered, not scientific knowledge supposedly reduced and concentrated, but some real, integrated, and articulate, though imperfect, understanding—what Plato would have called "right opinion"—about the nature and meaning of that knowledge which is proper to men in possession of the intellectual virtues. Moreover, at the same time, the youth can get a few basic insights into the main acquisitions with which this knowledge has provided the human mind. Education must never give up the idea of universal knowledge, but it must realize all the practical implications of this principle that universal knowledge is possible only at a non-scientific level, at the level of natural intelligence, not at the level of science and the intellectual virtues. Universal knowledge to be acquired by the youth at the level of natural intelligence is precisely the job of that which I consider essential for high-school and college years; namely, basic liberal education.[2]

Basic liberal education is liberal education directed to the natural intelligence of youth, with thorough respect for this intelligence, for its peculiar behavior still steeped in imagination, as well as for its need for unity, but with no pretension to go beyond it and enter the sphere proper to the intellectual virtues. The genuine task is neither encyclopedic inculcation nor what I should like to call nursery accommodation: it is basic liberal education, dealing with universal knowledge at the level of natural intelligence and using natural intelligence's own approach.

EDUCATIONAL AIMS AND VALUES

THE AIMS OF EDUCATION

Concerning Philosophical Principles. The primary aim of education in the broadest sense of this word is to "form a man" or, rather, to help a child of man attain his full formation or his completeness as a man. The other aims (to convey the heritage of culture of a given area of civilization, to prepare for life in society and for good citizenship, and to secure the mental equipment required for implementing a particu-

---

[2] It is because he misses the notion of basic liberal education that Professor Boas, who takes pleasure in assailing the "mythological monster known as the cultivated man" thinks that in the space of a four-year college education a student cannot attain this goal. (Ann Arbor Conference of Higher Education. Cf. New York *Times*, November 26, 1952.) He would be right *if* college education had to achieve its task at the level of *science*, instead of at the level of *natural intelligence*.

lar function in the social whole, for performing family responsibilities, and for making a living) are corollaries and essential but secondary aims. (Parenthetically, it must be observed that education, in the broad sense of the word, continues during the entire lifetime of every one of us. The school system is only a *partial* and *inchoative* agency with respect to the task of education. Moreover, because it deals essentially with that which can be taught, it refers to the education and formation of intelligence more than of the will.)

It is clear that the primary aim is determined by human nature. The question "What is man?" is the unavoidable preamble to any philosophy of education. It has two implications: first, a philosophic or "ontological" implication, dealing with human nature in its essential being; second, a scientific or "empiriological" implication, dealing with human nature in the phenomenal characteristics that lie open to our modern sciences of observation and measurement. These two implications are in no way incompatible; they complement each other.

With respect to both the mind and the body, science, and especially empirical psychology, provides us with invaluable and ever-growing information, by which our practical approach to the child and the youth must profit. But, by itself, it can neither primarily found nor primarily guide education, for education needs primarily to know what man is—what are the constitutive principles of his being, what are his place and value in the world, what is his destiny. This has to do with the philosophical knowledge of man—including additional data which relate to his existential condition.

The Thomist idea of man coincides with the Greek, Jewish, and Christian idea: man as an animal endowed with reason, whose supreme dignity is in the intellect; and man as a free individual in personal relation with God, whose supreme righteousness consists in voluntarily obeying the law of God; and man as a sinful and wounded creature called to divine life and to the freedom of grace, whose supreme perfection consists in love.

At the same time, Thomist philosophy lays stress on the basic psychosomatic unity of the human being (one single substance composed of matter and a spiritual "form" or entelechy), thus affording us a philosophical key for a sound interpretation of great modern discoveries in neurology and psychiatry. Also, it lays stress on the notion of human personality. Man is a person, who holds himself in hand by his intelligence and his will. He does not exist merely as a physical being. There is in him a richer and nobler existence: he has spiritual superexistence, through knowledge and love. He is thus, in some way, a whole, and not merely a part; he is a universe unto himself, a microcosm in which the great universe can be encompassed through knowledge. Through love he can give himself freely to beings who are to him, as it were, other selves; and for this relationship no equivalent can be found in the physical world.

Man evolves in history. Yet his nature as such, his place and value in the cosmos, his dignity, his rights and aspirations as a person, and his destiny do not change. Consequently, the secondary aims of education have to be adjusted to changing conditions in successive historical periods; but as concerns the primary aim, as well as the intrinsic domination it exercises on the secondary aims, it is sheer illusion to speak of a ceaseless reconstruction of the aims of education.

Concerning Practical Application. Human nature does not change, but our knowledge of it may be philosophically warped or inadequate. Moreover, this knowledge steadily progresses in the field of the factual and empiriological sciences.

The philosophical knowledge of man which reigned as a rule in the last three centuries was basically Cartesian, and Thomist philosophy is strongly opposed both to Cartesian dualism and to the idealist and narrowly rationalistic bias it made prevalent in education. On the other hand, while shifting toward a philosophical outlook which is equally warped, but in the opposite way (the empiricist, positivist, or materialist bias), our epoch witnesses outstanding progress in the experimental sciences of man.

Accordingly I would say that both in its reaction against Cartesian rationalism and its heedfulness of the achievements of modern psychology, progressive education provides us with invaluable improvements. Our understanding of the realities connected with the aims of education has become truer and deeper. For example, due attention has been paid to the unconscious, the instincts, the nonrational elements in the psyche of the child. At the same time, educational techniques are in a process of continual broadening and enriching, so that it is right to speak of a ceaseless reconstruction of the *means* of education, so long as such reconstruction does not indulge in errors deriving from pseudophilosophical extrapolation, like the overemphasis on sex and sexual complexes, due to cheap psychology and spurious Freudianism, or the "cultural epoch" theory of G. Stanley Hall which would allow free rein to be given to the instincts of the child who they imagine will come to civilization through savagery. The greatest attention must be paid in this connection to Piaget's experiments and similar researches, and to renewals in the educational approach, such as those advocated by Montessori.

THE HIERARCHY OF VALUES

Concerning Philosophical Principles. There is no unity or integration without a stable hierarchy of values. Now in the true hierarchy of values, according to Thomist philosophy, knowledge and love of what is above time are superior to, and embrace and quicken, knowledge and love of what is within time. Charity, which loves God and embraces all men in this very love, is the supreme virtue. In the intellectual realm, wisdom, which knows things eternal and creates order and unity in the mind, is superior to science or to knowledge through particular causes; and the speculative intellect, which knows for the sake of knowing, comes before the practical intellect, which knows for the sake of action. In such a hierarchy of values, what is infravalent is not sacrificed to, but kept alive by, what is supravalent, because everything is appendant to faith in truth. Aristotle was right in sensing that contemplation is in itself better than action and more fitted to what is the most spiritual in man, but Aristotelian contemplation was purely intellectual and theoretical, while Christian contemplation, being rooted in love, superabounds in action.

Education obviously does not have to make of the child or the youth a scientist, a sage, and a contemplative. Yet, if the word "contemplation" is taken in its original and simplest sense (to contemplate is simply to *see* and to enjoy seeing), leaving aside its highest—metaphysical or religious—connotations, it must be said that knowledge is contemplative in nature, and that education, in its final and highest achievements, tends to develop the contemplative capacity of the human mind. It does so neither in order to have the mind come to a stop in the act of knowing and contemplating, nor in order to make knowledge and contemplation subservient to action, but in order that once man has reached a stage where the harmony of his inner energies has been brought to full completion, his action on the world and on the human community, and his creative power at the service of his fellow-men, may overflow from his contemplative contact with reality—both with the visible and invisible realities in the midst of which he lives and moves.

While dealing with the first steps in man's formation, education must itself be aware of the genuine hierarchy of intellectual values, be guided by such awareness in its task of preparation, preserve in the youth the natural germs of what is best in the life of the mind, and equip them with the beginnings of those disciplines of knowledge which matter most to man. It is a pity to see so many young people bewildered by highly developed and specialized, but chaotic, instruction about anything whatever in the field of particular sciences and miserably ignorant of everything that concerns God and the deepest realities in man and the world. What we are faced with, in this regard, is a kind of regular frustration—by adults and the general organization of teaching—of certain of the most vital needs and aspirations, and even of the basic rights, of intellectual nature in young persons.

Concerning Practical Application. One of the vices of the sort of education described in the Lynds' *Middletown*[3] was not only to treat the child as a piece of inert matter to be molded from the outside but also to try to make him into a reduction or imitation of an adult, a kind of perfect manufactured intellectual dwarf. Hence, the prevalence of a merely theoretical and abstract formation, in accordance with an ideal of the adult man himself which, by the most confusing abuse of language, is often described as "contemplative," though it has nothing to do with genuine contemplative virtues, and refers in actual fact to that particular selfishness of the mind which comes about when intelligence is both separated from things—occupied only with handling and moving ideas and words—and separated from the emotional and affective tonus of life. This ideal was in its heyday during the seventeenth and eighteenth centuries. It was far removed from the Aristotelian one; it originated, philosophically, in Cartesian rationalism and, socially, in a trend, among the élite, toward a kind of lofty Epicurean freedom. According to it, the enviable condition of the man of leisure was to sit down before the spectacle of the achievements of the human mind and to taste the pleasure of "general ideas" without engaging either his heart or his intellect in the reality of things.

[3] Robert S. Lynd and Helen M. Lynd, *Middletown: A Study of Contemporary American Culture* (New York: Harcourt, Brace & Co.), 1929.

Out of gear as it may have been, the pragmatist protest against such an attitude was sound in its origin. Concern for action and practical life was to be rehabilitated in education. The misfortune was that the true hierarchy of values was broken at the same time. We have to integrate many views of pragmatism and progressive education—but at their appropriate place, which is secondary, and as regards especially the ways and means of education—in a nonpragmatist conception intent on the organic order of knowledge and directed toward wisdom.

As I pointed out above,[4] the order of human virtues come to completion demands that practical action on the world and on the human community superabound from contemplation of truth, which means not only contemplation in its purest forms but, more generally, intellectual grasping of reality and enjoyment of knowledge for its own sake. But in the educational process, what we have to do with is not human life as come to perfection; it is the very first beginnings of the lifelong movement toward such an ultimate stage. Then the perspective is reversed. Action must come first—and concern for application, practical significance, and the impact of the things which are taught on man's existence—not for action itself as final end, but in order to awaken progressively the child and the youth to seek and perceive truth for the sake of truth, to exercise their power to think, and to sense the joy of intellection. *From praxis to knowledge*, this is the normal method of education, especially in its first steps.

EDUCATIONAL PROCESS

The remarks I just made about action must be qualified on a particular point: if it is a question of the atmosphere of the classroom, contemplation, in a sense, and especially as

4 See *supra*, pp. 53-54.

regards young children, should come first; in Montessorian classes, which obey the two fundamental rules of *silence* and *personal effort*, the behavior of children changes completely; they move as they work, but with no agitation, and become so concentrated and so absorbed in their task that the visitor in these noiseless classrooms is surprised to have the impression of a monastic climate. Hélène Lubienska de Lenval observes that these children simply reveal, in an appropriate environment, the contemplative capacity peculiar to early childhood (ages two to eight). They are contemplative, as she puts it, "in the sense that they are capable of steadily fixing their attention by absorbing themselves in a disinterested admiration with no verbal manifestation (the latter will arise in due time after a long silent maturation). This contemplation seems akin to poetic inspiration." And because "it comes about most often before objects that represent dimensions and numbers," she calls it "Pythagorean contemplation."[5] This contemplative faculty of the child is ephemeral; it disappears at the moment when discursive thought replaces intuitive thought. But something of it remains, for those who once enjoyed it show remarkable powers of attention in later years.

If we pass now to the question of learning by way of solving problems, I would say that this method of learning is normally a way to truth-grasping or "contemplative" learning, just as *praxis* is a way to knowledge. It is a normal auxiliary means, destined to sustain personal initiative and interest, and to prevent contemplative learning from degenerating into passivity and inert docility. For there is no contemplative learning if it does not respond to and stimulate a searching effort of the mind, an anxiety to know. Truth, in education, can be betrayed in two ways: either by substituting mechanical drill, and skill in solving difficulties, for the *élan* toward knowledge; or by putting the intellect of the

---

[5] Hélène Lubienska de Lenval, "La Contemplation Silencieuse Chez les Enfants," *Nova et Vetera* (Fribourg, Switzerland). July–September, 1951.

student to sleep in ready-made formulas, which he accepts
and memorizes without engaging his own self in the grasping
of what they supposedly convey to him. Genuine contemplative or truth-grasping learning fails in its very nature if it
does not develop in the youth both critical activity and a
kind of thirst and anguish whose reward will be the very joy
of perceiving truth.

But, in this section on the educational process, the point I
should like especially to consider is the relationship between
adults and youth.

In the educational task, adult people do not have to impose coercion on children, with a kind of paternalism or
rather imperialism of the grown-ups, in order to impress their
own image upon the child as upon a bit of clay. But what
this service requires from them is, first, love and, then, authority—I mean genuine authority, not arbitrary power—
intellectual authority to teach and moral authority to be
respected and listened to. For the child is entitled to expect
from them what he needs: to be positively guided and to
learn what he does not know.

What do adults essentially owe to youth in the educational
task? First of all, what corresponds to the primary aim of
education, that is, both truth to be known at the various degrees of the scale of knowledge and the capacity to think
and make a personal judgment, to be developed, equipped,
and firmly established; then, what corresponds to the secondary aims of education, especially the heritage of a given
culture, to be conveyed.

Now, if we consider the way in which adults perform their
task with respect to youth, in practice and actual existence,
it seems that more often than not children are victims of the
grown-ups rather than the beneficiaries of their good services. Hence, progressive education might be described as expressing a kind of revolt against the reign of adults. This
would have been all for the good if youth had not been
made, once again, a victim, this time not of the selfish domi-

nation of the world of grown-ups, but of the illusions and irresponsibility of well-intentioned adults, who rightly insist on the freedom of the child—but what kind of freedom? Too often freedom from any rule, or freedom to do as the child pleases, instead of genuine freedom for the child to develop as a man and genuine progress toward autonomy.

A twofold crucial problem arises when the educational task has to be performed in a changing world of knowledge and a changing world of cultural and social conditions.

As concerns the social changes in the contemporary world, teachers have neither to make the school into a stronghold of the established order nor to make it into a weapon to change society. The dilemma would not be solved if the primary aim and function of education were defined in relation to society and social work. In reality they are defined in relation to intelligence. Then the dilemma is transcended because teachers must be concerned, above all, with helping minds to become articulate, free, and autonomous. It is neither for conservative nor for revolutionary purposes, but for the general purpose of teaching how to think, that they have to foster in the pupils the principles of the democratic charter.

As concerns our changing world of knowledge, the answer is simple in itself: *vetera novis augere;* all new gains and discoveries should be used, not to shatter and reject what has been acquired by the past, but to augment it: a work of integration, not of destruction. This, however, is easier said than done. For it presupposes that the mind of the adults, especially the teachers', is not itself in a state of division and anarchy, and that the adults are in possession of what they have to communicate, namely, wisdom and integrated knowledge. Not to speak of exceptionally remarkable achievements in interdepartmental co-operation like the Committee on Social Thought in the University of Chicago, one possible remedy for the lack of integration in the minds of teachers themselves would be, in my opinion, the development, on a large scale, of study clubs and seminars in which teachers belonging to various disciplines and departments would meet together, on a voluntary basis, and discuss basic problems which are relevant to the unity of knowledge and which have an impact on a variety of fields, as well as controversial issues that are raised by contemporary research and creative activity. I am convinced that it would thus be possible for fresh and quickening blood to circulate in the campuses. But such initiative could obviously start and succeed only if teachers had the necessary free time, that is to say, if they were not faced with overburdened schedules and a much too heavy number of teaching hours—one of the most serious impediments to the progress of the present educational system. It is preposterous to ask people who lead an enslaved life to perform a task of liberation, which the educational task is by essence.

EDUCATION AND THE INDIVIDUAL

Concerning Philosophical Principles. Among the many questions which can be discussed under this heading, the one I shall point out is the essential question: Who is the "principal agent" in the educational process?

The teacher exercises a real causal power on the mind of the pupil, but in the manner in which a doctor acts to heal his patient: by assisting nature and co-operating with it. Education, like medicine, is *ars cooperativa naturae.* The contention of Thomist philosophy is that in both cases nature (the vital energies of nature in the patient, the intellectual energies of nature in the pupil) is the principal agent, on whose own activity the process primarily depends. The *principal agent* in the educational process is not the teacher, but the student.[6]

Concerning Practical Application. This basic truth was

[6] Cf. Thomas Aquinas, *Sum. Theol.,* I, q. 117, a. 1; *Contra Gent.,* Bk. II, chap. lxxv; *De Verit.,* q. 11, a. 1.

forgotten or disregarded by the advocates of education by the rod. Here we have the fundamental vice of the "Middletown" conception of the school. Into whatever exaggeration it may have fallen, progressive education has had the merit of putting the forgotten truth in question in the foreground. The "principal agent" is not able to give himself what he does not have. He would lead himself astray if he acted at random. He must be taught and guided: But the main thing in this teaching process is that his natural and spontaneous activity be always respected and his power of insight and judgment always fostered, so that at each step he may master the subject matter in which he is instructed. In this perspective, what matters most is to develop in the child the "intuitivity" of the mind and its spiritual discriminating and creative energies. The educational venture is a ceaseless appeal to intelligence and free will in the young person.

The most precious gift in an educator is a sort of sacred and loving attention to the child's mysterious identity, which is a hidden thing that no techniques can reach. Encouragement is as fundamentally necessary as humiliation is harmful. But what must be specially stressed is the fact that the teacher has to center the acquisition of knowledge and solid formation of the mind on the freeing of the learner's intuitive power.

The liberation of which I am speaking depends essentially, moreover, on the free adhesion of the mind to the objective reality to be seen: "Let us never deceive or rebuke the thirst for seeing in youth's intelligence! The freeing of the intuitive power is achieved in the soul through the object grasped, the intelligible grasping toward which this power naturally tends. The germ of insight starts within a preconscious intellectual cloud, arising from experience, imagination, and a kind of spiritual feeling, but it is from the outset a tending toward an object to be grasped. And to the extent that this tendency is set free and the intellect becomes accustomed to grasping, seeing, expressing the objects toward which it tends, to that very extent its intuitive power is liberated and strengthened."[7]

In asking a youth to read a book, let us get him to undertake a real spiritual adventure and meet and struggle with the internal world of a given man, instead of glancing over a collection of bits of thought and dead opinions, looked upon from without and with sheer indifference, according to the horrible custom of so many victims of what they call "being informed." Perhaps with such methods the curriculum will lose a little in scope, which will be all to the good.[8]

SCHOOL AND SOCIETY

THE TEACHING OF THE DEMOCRATIC CHARTER

Concerning Philosophical Principles. A society of free men implies agreement between minds and wills on the bases of life in common. There are, thus, a certain number of tenets—about the dignity of the human person, human rights, human equality, freedom, justice, and law—about which democracy presupposes common consent and which constitute what may be called the democratic charter. Without a general, firm, and reasoned-out conviction concerning such tenets, democracy cannot survive.

But these basic tenets and this charter of freedom are of a strictly *practical* character—at the point of convergence of the theoretical approaches peculiar to the various, even opposite, schools of thought which are rooted in the history of modern nations. No common assent can be required by society regarding the *theoretical justifications*, the conceptions of the world and of life, the philosophical or religious creeds which found, or claim to found, the practical tenets of the

[7] *Education at the Crossroads*, p. 44.
[8] *Ibid.*, pp. 44–45.

democratic charter. A genuine democracy cannot impose on its citizens or demand from them, as a condition for their belonging to the city, any philosophic or any religious creed. As a result, as I have pointed out elsewhere:

The body politic has the right and the duty to promote among its citizens, mainly through education, the human and temporal—and essentially practical—creed on which depend national communion and civil peace. It has no right, as a merely temporal or secular body, to impose on the citizens or to demand from them a rule of faith or a conformism of reason, a philosophical or religious creed which would present itself as the only possible justification of the practical charter through which the people's common secular faith expresses itself. The important thing for the body politic is that the democratic sense be in fact kept alive by the adherence of minds, however diverse, to this moral charter. The ways and the justifications by means of which this common adherence is brought about pertain to the freedom of minds and consciences.[9]

Since education (one of the essential, though secondary, aims of which is to prepare for life in society and good citizenship) is obviously the primary means to foster common conviction in the democratic charter, a particularly serious and difficult problem arises at this point for educational philosophy.

On the one hand, the educational system has a duty to see to the teaching of the charter of freedom. Yet it can do this only in the name of the common assent through which the charter in question is held true by the people. And thus —since in actual fact the body politic is divided in its fundamental theoretical conceptions, and since the democratic state cannot impose any philosophical or religious creed— the educational system, in seeing to the teaching of the common charter, can and must cling only to the common prac-

[9] Jacques Maritain, *Man and the State* (Chicago: University of Chicago Press, 1951), pp. 111–12.

tical recognition of the merely practical tenets upon which the people have agreed to live together, despite the diversity or the opposition between their spiritual traditions and schools of thought.

On the other hand, there is no belief except in what is held to be intrinsically established in truth, nor any assent of the intellect without a theoretical foundation and justification. Thus, if the educational system is to perform its duty and inculcate the democratic charter in a really efficacious way, it cannot help resorting to the philosophical or religious traditions and schools of thought which are spontaneously at work in the consciousness of the nation and which have contributed historically to its formation.

Adherence to one or another of those schools of thought rests with the freedom of each person. But it would be sheer illusion to think that the democratic charter could be efficiently taught if it were separated from the roots that give it consistency and vigor in the mind of youth, and if it were reduced to a mere series of abstract formulas—bookish, bloodless, and cut off from life. Those who teach the democratic charter must stake on it their personal convictions, their consciences, and the depth of their moral lives. They must, therefore, explain and justify its articles in the light of the philosophical or religious faith to which they cling and which quickens their belief in it.

Now, if every teacher does thus put all his philosophical or religious convictions, his personal faith, and his soul into the effort to confirm and vivify the moral charter of democracy, then it is clear that such teaching demands a certain spontaneous adaptation between the one who gives and the one who receives, between the aspiration animating the teacher and the basic conceptions that the student holds from his home circle and his social milieu and that his family feels the duty of fostering and developing in him.[10]

[10] *Ibid.*, pp. 121–22.

The conclusion is obvious. For the very sake of providing unity in adherence to the democratic charter, a sound pluralism must obtain in the means. Inner differentiations must come into force in the structure of the educational system, which must admit within itself pluralistic patterns enabling teachers to put their entire convictions and most personal inspiration in their teaching of the democratic charter.

Concerning Practical Application with Respect to the Teaching of the Democratic Charter. After having put forward general views quite akin to those I have just mentioned, Mahan states:

> I think we can set down one principle as basic: that public schools must recognize and acknowledge the various influences, both religious and areligious, which inspired our democratic ideal. . . . That principle is very broad and gives rise to seemingly insurmountable problems. How are we going to insure unbiased exposition of influence? There are several ways—none of them very practical.[11]

I am ready to admit that no perfectly satisfactory solution can be found. In such a complex matter, some inherent difficulty or questionable aspect may always be pointed out. Nevertheless I keep on believing that prudential wisdom can invent and apply solutions which—though more or less imperfect in some respect—will prove to be the best possible under given circumstances.

I would like, first, to remark that any teacher entrusted with the teaching of the democratic charter should possess two complementary qualities: on the one hand, he should be animated, as we have seen, by deep personal convictions, in which his whole philosophy of life is engaged—for no teaching deprived of conviction can engender conviction; on the other hand, he should have such intellectual openness

[11] Thomas W. Mahan, "The Problem of a Democratic Philosophy of Education," *School and Society*, LXXVI (September 7, 1952), 193–96.

and generosity as to foster a sense of fellowship with respect to those who justify the democratic creed through other theoretical approaches—this is required, as we have seen, by the very nature of the thing taught. And this, moreover, is of a nature to lessen to some extent the difficulty of our problem, when it comes to minorities which do not share in the philosophical or religious outlook of the teacher, and which, of course, must not be discriminated against.

Now there are, in my opinion as regards practical application, three possible ways which might be submitted for consideration.

In the first place, we might imagine that when the schools are located in communities each one of which is homogeneous as to its spiritual traditions, the teachers who are in charge of the democratic charter could be allotted such or such a particular area, according to their own wishes as well as to the moral geography of the local communities, so that their own personal religious or philosophical convictions would roughly correspond to those which prevail in the social environment.

In the second place, when the local communities in which schools are located are heterogeneous as to their spiritual traditions, the teaching of the democratic charter might be divided among a few different teachers whose respective personal outlooks correspond in broad outline to the main religious or philosophical traditions represented in the student population.

In the third place, instead of having the democratic charter taught as a special part of the curriculum, we might have it embodied in a new discipline which would be introduced into the curriculum, and which, being merely historical, would permit the teacher, while giving a free rein to his personal inspiration, to put less emphasis on the theoretical principles which justify for him the secular democratic faith. The new discipline in question would bring together, in the basic framework of national history and history of civilization, matters pertaining to the humanities, human sciences, social philosophy, and philosophy of law, all these to be centered on the development and significance of the great ideas comprised in the common charter. Thus, this charter would be taught in a concrete and comprehensive manner, in the light of the great poets, thinkers, and heroes of mankind, of our knowledge of man, and of the historical life of the nation.

Would the three ways I just mentioned answer all the requirements of the practical issue under discussion? They are, it seems to me, at least worthy of being tentatively tried and tested. They are the only ways I am able to conceive of, but I hope that other and better ones can be proposed. In any case the fact remains that the teaching of the democratic charter is, today, one of the chief obligations of education and no practical solution is possible except along the lines of some pluralistic arrangement.

Americans may disagree as to why American democracy is right, but they must agree that there are reasons why it is right. I do not know how public education can meet the demand upon it to insure that conviction. I do know that, if the public schools are allowed to swallow the philosophy of scientific humanism because of its purported neutrality, they will fail to meet their obligations to further the common good.[12]

Concerning Practical Application with Respect to School Life. From the point of view of practical application, there are other considerations whose relevance should be stressed as regards the preparation of the youth for a real understanding of the democratic way of life. These considerations no longer have to do with the teaching; they have rather to do with the very life of the school and the college.

[12] Thomas W. Mahan, *loc. cit.*, p. 196.

There, in the life of the school and the college, the beginnings of the habits and virtues of freedom and responsibility should take place in actual exercise. In other words, the students should not be a merely receptive element in the life of that kind of republic which is the school or the college. They should, to some extent, actively participate in it. The best way for this would obtain, in my opinion, if they were freely organized in teams, responsible for the discipline of their members and their progress in work.

Such an experiment was made in some places with surprisingly good results. The teams are formed by the students themselves, without any interference from school authorities; they elect their own captains; they have regular meetings—which no teacher attends—in which they examine and discuss how the group behaves and the questions with which it is confronted. Their captains, on the other hand, as representatives of each team, have regular contacts with the school authorities, to whom they convey the suggestions, experiences, and problems of the group. So the students are actually interested in the organization of studies, the general discipline, the "political life" of the school or the college, and they can play a sort of consultative part in the activity of the educational republic.

With such methods, the youth become concretely aware of, and attached to, the democratic way of life, while a sense of dignity and self-discipline, collective autonomy, and collective honor develops in them. In a manner adapted to the age and capacity of students, schools and universities should be laboratories in the responsibilities of freedom and the qualities of the mind proper to democratic citizenship. It can hardly be stated that no improvement is needed in this respect. Displays of oratory, making students proud of their skill in airing opinions, and intoxicated with words, seem to me to be only illusory compensations for the lack to which I just alluded.

LIBERAL EDUCATION FOR ALL

Concerning Philosophical Principles. Education directed toward wisdom, centered on the humanities, aiming to develop in people the capacity to think correctly and to enjoy truth and beauty, is education for freedom, or liberal education. Whatever his particular vocation may be, and whatever special training his vocation may require, every human being is entitled to receive such a properly human and humanistic education.

Liberal education was restricted in the past to the children of the upper classes. This very fact reacted on the way in which it was itself conceived. Liberal education for all obliges us, I believe, to undertake a double reconsideration.

In the first place, a serious recasting of the very concept of the humanities and the liberal arts has been made necessary by the development of human knowledge in modern centuries. The notion of the humanistic disciplines and the field of liberal arts must be enlarged so as to comprise physics and the natural sciences, the history of sciences, anthropology and the other human sciences, with the history of cultures and civilizations, even technology (insofar as the activity of the spirit is involved), and the history of manual work and the arts, both mechanical and fine arts.

I would like to insist, in particular, that physics and the natural sciences must be considered one of the chief branches of the liberal arts. They are mainly concerned with the mathematical reading of natural phenomena, and they insure in this way the domination of the human spirit over the world of matter, not in terms of ontological causes but rather in terms of number and measurement. Thus they appear, so to speak, as a final realization of the Pythagorean and Platonist trends of thought in the very field of that world of *experience* and *becoming* which Plato looked upon as a shadow on the wall of the cave. Physics and the natural sciences, if they are taught not only for the sake of practical applications but essentially for the sake of knowledge, provide man with a vision of the universe and a sense of the sacred, exacting, unbending objectivity of the humblest truth, which play an essential part in the liberation of the mind and in liberal education. Physics, like mathematics, if it is viewed as the creative power from which great discoveries proceed, is close to poetry. If it were taught as it demands to be, in the light of the spiritual workings of man, it should be revered as a liberal art of the first rank and an integral part of the humanities.

As to the human sciences, the positivistic bias with which, as a rule, they are cultivated today makes their humanistic value rather questionable indeed. Yet this is an abnormal situation, for which they themselves are not responsible. It would be a great misfortune, and a blunder, to exclude from the realm of the humanities the sciences of man, even though developed at the level of empiriological knowledge. The problem for them, as for physics and the other sciences of phenomena, is to be set free, in the minds of scientists, from the pseudo-philosophical prejudices which have preyed upon them as parasites. They should be taught, insofar as they are a part of a program in the humanities, from a philosophical point of view, with reference to the particular epistemological approach they involve, and with a constant concern either for the understanding of human nature and the development of its potentialities, or for the understanding of the ways in which the human mind functions.

We have also to stress the crucial importance of the history of sciences with respect to humanistic education. In the perspective of the humanities, the genesis of science in the human mind and its progress, adventures, and vicissitudes in the course of history have as much illuminating power as the results that science attains and the changing disclosures on the universe of nature that it offers us in various periods of its development. Knowledge of the succession of scientific theories, of the inner logic, and also of the part of chance and contingency that can be observed in their evolution, and of the actual ways through which scientific imagination proceeds from discovery to discovery can alone give the student a real understanding of scientific truth and its authentic range. The history of sciences is the genuine instrument through which the physical sciences can be integrated in the humanities and their humanistic value brought out in full light.

In the second place, it has become indispensable to give full recognition to the concept of basic liberal education and to the typical requirements it involves. I have just indicated the necessary *broadening* of the *matters* comprised within the scope of the liberal arts and the humanities. What I am now emphasizing is the necessary *restriction* of the burden imposed on the student, and of the curriculum, as concerns the very *ways and perspective* in which the matters in question have to be taught.

Let us refer to the considerations laid down in a previous section on natural intelligence and basic liberal education.[13] On the one hand, the objective of basic liberal education is not the acquisition of science itself or of art itself, along with the intellectual virtues involved, but rather the grasp of their *meaning* and the comprehension of the truth and beauty they yield. We grasp the meaning of a science or an art when we understand its object, nature, and scope, and the particular species of truth or beauty it discloses to us. The objective of basic liberal education is to see to it that the young person grasps this truth or beauty through the natural powers and gifts of his mind and the natural intuitive energy of his reason backed up by his whole sensuous, imaginative, and emotional dynamism.

On the other hand, as concerns the content of knowledge,

[13] See *supra,* pp. 48–50.

of the *things* that the young person has to learn, this content is to be determined by the very requirements of the grasp in question. Many things which were taught in the past in liberal education are useless; many things which were not taught in the past in liberal education are necessary in this regard. But in any case, the subjects and methods which are proper to graduate studies have no place at this level. In short, the guiding principle is less factual information and more intellectual enjoyment. The teaching should be concentrated on awakening the minds to a few basic intuitions or intellectual perceptions in each particular discipline, through which what is essentially illuminating as to the truth of things learned is definitely and unshakably possessed. The result would be both a rise in quality of the teaching received and an alleviation of the material burden imposed by the curriculum.

Concerning Practical Application. If all the preceding remarks are true, we see that the distinction between basic liberal education and higher learning or graduate studies should be emphasized: because the first deals with a world of knowledge appropriate to natural intelligence, the second with a world of knowledge appropriate to intellectual virtues.

When he enters this world of knowledge proper to higher learning, or the world of technical and professional studies, or the world of practical activity in a given job, the youth will specialize in a particular field. At the same time he will have the opportunity, either by means of the university or the technological institutions, or by his own initiative, to pursue and improve his humanistic education. This would be simply impossible if he were not previously equipped with an adequate basic liberal education.

Basic liberal education should cover both high school and college. During high-school years, the mode of teaching would be adapted to the freshness and spontaneous curiosity of budding reason, stirred and nourished by the life of the imagination. When it comes to college years, we would have to do with natural intelligence in a state of growth, with its full natural aspirations to universal knowledge—and, at the same time, with its normal tendency to develop some more perfect *habitus* or disposition relating to preparation for a particular field of activity. So the college would have to insure both basic liberal education in its final stages and the development of a particular state of capacity. The best arrangement for this purpose would be to have the college divided into a number of fields of concentration or fields of primary interest, each one represented by a given school (or *institut*, in the French sense of this word). In effect, this would be to have the college divided into a number of *schools of oriented humanities*, all of which would be dedicated to basic liberal education, but each of which would be concerned with preparatory study in a particular field of activity, thus dealing with the beginnings and first development of a given intellectual virtue or a given intellectual skill. And basic liberal education rather than this preparatory study would be the primary aim. But precisely in order to make basic liberal education fully efficacious, the manner in which it would be given, and the teaching organized, would take into consideration the particular intellectual virtue, or the particular intellectual skill, to be developed in the future scientist or businessman, artist, doctor, newspaperman, teacher, lawyer, or specialist in government.

I mean that all the students would have to attend courses in all the matters of the curriculum in basic liberal education; but, on the one hand, the apportionment of the hours given to certain of these courses might be different for the students in the various schools of oriented humanities; and, on the other hand, special courses in each of these schools would enlighten the student on the vital relationship between the particular discipline being taught and the chief disciplines of the common curriculum.

Thus, the essential hierarchy of values inherent in liberal education would be preserved, with the main emphasis, as to the disciplines, on philosophy; and, as to the ways and methods, on the reading of great books. But the practical arrangement of the curriculum would be attuned, in the manner I just indicated, to what will be later on, in actual fact, the principal activity of the person who is now a student. In this way it would be easier to insure the unity and integration of the teaching, especially if the teachers of each school of oriented humanities co-operated in a close and constant manner so as to elaborate and enforce a common educational policy. And the students would receive a kind of pre-professional training (unavoidable as it is in actual existence) which, instead of impairing liberal education and worming its way into it like a parasite, would serve to make the young person more vitally interested in liberal education and more deeply penetrated by it.

The notion of basic liberal education, with the kind of re-casting of the list of liberal arts and the method of teaching the humanities we have considered, is of a nature, it seems to me, to give practical and existential value to the concept of *liberal education for all.* On the one hand, basic liberal education, dealing only with the sphere of knowledge and the educational approach appropriate to natural intelligence and respecting the need of natural intelligence for unity and integration, avoids any burden of pseudo-science to be imposed on the student and feeds on the spontaneous, natural interests of his mind. On the other hand, given the broadening of the field of liberal arts and humanities, on the necessity of which I have laid stress, liberal education would cease being considered an almost exclusively literary education. Since the humanities in our age of culture require articulate knowledge of the achievements of the human mind in science as well as in literature and art, and since it is normal to attune, during college years, the common teaching of the humanities, essential for all, to a particular preparatory training diversified according to the various prospective vocations of the students, basic liberal education is adapted to all the real needs which the liberal education of the past was reproached with being unable to satisfy.

Basic liberal education does not look upon students as future professors or specialists in all the branches of knowledge and the liberal arts taught in the curriculum. It does not look upon them as future gentlemen or members of the privileged class. It looks upon them as future citizens, who must act as free men and who are able to make sound and independent judgments in new and changing situations, either with respect to the body politic or to their own particular task. It is also to be expected that these future citizens would educate their children and discuss with them competently the matters taught in school. Moreover, it is assumed that they would dedicate their own leisure time to those activities of rest through which man enjoys the common heritage of knowledge and beauty, or those activities of superabundance through which he helps his fellow-men with generosity.

SCHOOL AND RELIGION

MORAL EDUCATION AND RELIGION

Concerning Philosophical Principles. Formation in moral life and virtues is an essential part, indeed the most important part, of the primary aim of education in the broad sense of the word. School and college education is not equipped to secure it in a full and complete manner; yet it is bound to contribute positively and efficaciously to the moral formation of the youth.

This depends a great deal on the general inspiration of the teaching, especially on the way in which study in the humanities and the reading of the works of great poets and writers convey to young people the treasure of moral ideas and moral experience of mankind. Yet the assistance of religious education is basically needed. It is a fact that we live in the Judaeo-Christian tradition. And, over and above all, it is a fundamental human datum that moral life, in one way or another, sometimes unconsciously, is linked with religious belief and experience. If the existence of the One who is the Absolute Being and the Absolute Good is not recognized and believed in, no certitude in the unconditional and obligatory value of moral law and ethical standards can be validly established and efficaciously adhered to.

It is, therefore, an obligation for the school and the college not only to enlighten students on moral matters, but also to allow them to receive full religious education.

Concerning Practical Application. The practical problem has to do with secular (nondenominational) schools and universities and with state institutions. It might be said that the lay character of the curriculum or the matters of learning (what is called in French *instruction,* in contradistinction to *éducation*) in the modern school system corresponds to the lay character of the modern state. This does not prevent religious inspiration, if the teachers have any, in the teaching of these matters any more than it prevents religious inspiration in civil life. It only prevents secular institutions from dogmatizing in religious matters and taking a stand in favor of any particular religious denomination.

A sharp distinction between church and state does not mean that the church and the state must live in ignorance of and isolation from each other. On the contrary, they have to co-operate. But this distinction means that the proper domain of the state is lay or secular and that no privileged treatment, contrary to the principle of the equality of all before the law, can be given by the state to the citizens of any given creed, their activities, or their institutions.

Accordingly, the solution, in the educational sphere, is to be sought in a sound application of the pluralist principle. Religious training should be made available to the student population—not in a compulsory way, but on a voluntary basis—in accordance with the wishes of the students and their parents, and given by representatives of the various faiths.

Shall I run counter to the conventions of contemporary education if I add that this religious training should not only be received from the family and the church community, independently of the life of the school, but should also be connected with this very life as an integral part thereof? In any case, this is my own conviction. If we are firmly and positively persuaded that religion is but error and superstition, this conviction will of course appear to us as nonsense; yet, in such a case we have no right to impose our own areligious or irreligious philosophy on our fellow-citizens; we do have the right to shun religious training for our own children and to have them attend courses in good manners and civic morality or enjoy scientific entertainment, while the other students listen to their respective teachers in religion. But if we do not hold religion to be error and superstition, I do not see how we can assume that God is less entitled to have His place in the school than the electron or Professor Bertrand Russell.

All serious-minded observers agree that the split between religion and life is the root of the spiritual disorder from which we suffer today. It is preposterous to make this split begin in childhood and to perpetuate it in the educational system by cutting off religious training from the training proper to schools and colleges. Young people are aware of the fact that school and college education is in charge of furnishing their minds with each and every knowledge required by the realities of life. If religious knowledge is disconnected from this education, it is normal to deem it something separate and additional, either superfluous or merely related to private sentimentality. It is the very right of the child and the youth to be equipped through his formal education with religious knowledge as well as with any knowledge which plays an essential part in the life of man.

Now if this solution, which, to my mind, is the normal one, is not accepted, secular schools and colleges should at least co-operate with the parents in giving the students who desire it appropriate free time and full facilities to be instructed in religious knowledge outside the school or the college, and to participate in extracurricular religious groups and activities. Those who are not interested in religion would use for cultural activities of their choice the free time thus granted to their fellow-students apart from curricular obligations.

THE TEACHING OF THEOLOGY

The moral aspect, furthermore, is far from being the only one to be considered in the issue we are discussing. Truth to be known about God and the relation of man to God matters more to religious faith than human actions to be regulated. In other words, it is not only in the moral perspective but also, and first of all, in the intellectual perspective and from the point of view of the full growth of the intellect that the issue must be examined. Then we are dealing with the interests of the intellect, that is to say, with what is the most immediate concern of school and college education. At this point it is relevant for me to state my views in terms of *theology* rather than of *religion*. For theology means knowledge *in the state of science*—a knowledge which is both rooted in revealed data and rationally developed, logically and systematically articulated. According to Thomas Aquinas, theology is both speculative and practical (or moral), but primarily speculative, and more speculative than practical. Anyone who believes in a divine revelation can hardly fail to hold with him that theology, which gives us some understanding of the divine mystery, is the highest wisdom that man can acquire as adapted to the procedures of human reason. It is superior to philosophy, which it employs as an appropriate instrument of rational disquisition, and is inferior only to contemplative or mystical wisdom.

How could the college be justified in doing without this wisdom while claiming fully to prepare and equip the minds of youth? No knowledge fit to fortify the mind and enlarge its scope can be absent from a place where universal knowledge is taught. For the believer, theology and theological controversy convey matters which are in themselves of supreme worth. For the unbeliever, they convey what a number of his fellow-men, at each step of an age-long civilized tradition, have fed on as matters of supreme worth. There may be unbelievers and believers together in the student population and in the teaching body of a university. But the university itself, as a living institution, cannot help taking a stand, and must take a stand, with respect to the existence of God. An atheist university, in which there is no teaching in theology, has intellectual consistency. A university which is not atheist, and in which there is no teaching in theology, has no intellectual consistency. Newman was right in stating that, if a university professes its scientific duty to exclude theology from its curriculum, "such an Institution cannot be what it professes, if there be a God."

As a matter of fact, as I pointed out in a book from which I take the liberty of quoting here:

Theological problems and controversies have permeated the whole development of Western culture and civilization, and are still at work in its depths, in such a way that the one who would ignore them would be fundamentally unable to grasp his own time and the meaning of its internal conflicts. Thus impaired, he would be like a barbarous and disarmed child walking amidst the queer and incomprehensible trees, fountains, statues, gardens, ruins, and buildings still under construction, of the old park of civilization. The intellectual and political history of the sixteenth, seventeenth, and eighteenth centuries, the Reformation and the Counter Reformation, the internal state of British society after the

Revolution in England, the achievements of the Pilgrim Fathers, the Rights of Man, and the further events in world history have their starting point in the great disputes on nature and grace of our classical age. Neither Dante nor Cervantes nor Rabelais nor Shakespeare nor John Donne nor William Blake, nor even Oscar Wilde nor D. H. Lawrence, nor Giotto nor Michelangelo nor El Greco nor Zurbaran, nor Pascal nor Rousseau, nor Madison nor Jefferson nor Edgar Allan Poe nor Baudelaire, nor Goethe nor Nietzsche nor even Karl Marx, nor Tolstoy nor Dostoevski is actually understandable without a serious theological background. Modern philosophy itself, from Descartes to Hegel, remains enigmatic without that, for in actual fact philosophy has burdened itself all through modern times with problems and anxieties taken over from theology, so that the cultural advent of a philosophy purely philosophical is still to be waited for. In the cultural life of the Middle Ages philosophy was subservient to theology or rather wrapped up in it; in that of modern times it was but secularized theology. Thus . . . liberal education cannot complete its task without the knowledge of the specific realm and the concerns of theological wisdom.[14]

The teaching of the latter should, moreover, be given in a quite different way from that appropriate to religious seminaries and be adapted to the intellectual needs of laymen; its aim should not be to form a priest, a minister, or a rabbi, but to enlighten students of secular matters about the great doctrines and perspectives of theological wisdom. Such teaching would not be concerned with the detailed apparatus of historical authorities, but it would rather lay stress on the intrinsic rational consistency of doctrines and the basic insights on which they depend. It would be free from any preoccupation with merely technical questions or dead quarrels and closely connected with the problems of contemporary science and culture. Studies in comparative religion would be included in it.

As far as practical application is concerned, it presents no

14 *Education at the Crossroads*, pp. 73–74.

difficulties for denominational colleges.[15] With regard to nondenominational colleges, the practical solution, here again, would depend on the recognition of the pluralist principle in such matters. "Theological teaching would be given, according to the diversity of creeds, by professors belonging to the main religious denominations, each one addressing the students of his own denomination. And of course, those students who nurture a bias against theology would be released from attending these courses and allowed to remain incomplete in wisdom at their own pleasure."[16]

THE INTEGRITY OF NATURAL REASON

A last observation must be made. Given the present situation of culture, the primary service that religion may receive from the school is that the school should restore in students the integrity of reason, of natural reason. As long as the teaching as a whole, in the high school as in college, is permeated with a general philosophy which relies only on sense experience and facts and figures, disintegrates reason and denies its proper perceptive power and the most valuable certainties of which the human intellect is capable—and the first of which is the rational knowledge of God's existence; as long as chaotic information is cultivated in the place of integrated knowledge and spiritual unity, the very soil and natural background on which religious convictions may thrive in youth will remain rough and barren.

Now, is the work of reason itself capable of taking on its full natural dimensions without the superior balance created in common consciousness by religious faith and inspiration? Is philosophy capable, in actual existence, of reaching its

[15] *Cf.* Gerald B. Phelan's indisputable statement on "Theology in the Curriculum of Catholic Colleges and Universities," in *Man and Secularism* (New York: National Catholic Alumni Association, 1940), pp. 128–40.

[16] *Education at the Crossroads*, p. 75.

own full rational integrity without the inner promptings and reinforcements it receives from theological knowledge? That is a major question, which I am only mentioning here. If we answer it in the affirmative, we have to say that human civilization, and its healing, depend on a complexity of causes which, as Aristotle put it, "cause one another." *Causae ad invicem sunt causae.*

In any case it would be nonsense to demand from teachers that they should be wiser than the general culture of their time and its great representatives, and that they should make up for the failure of the latter in doing the constructive work that mankind expected from them.

This means that the most crucial problem with which our educational system is confronted is not a problem of education, but of civilization.

Chapter Three

EDUCATION AND THE HUMANITIES

THE HUMANITIES AND THE WESTERN TRADITION

I take it for granted that education is not something aimless, it is not concerned with ceaselessly "reconstructing" its aims; and that the primary aim of education, in the broadest sense of this word, is to "form a man," or rather to help a child of man to attain his full formation or his completeness as a man. The other aims (namely, to convey the heritage of culture of a given area of civilization, to prepare for life in society and good citizenship, to secure mental equipment required for implementing a particular function in the social whole, performing family responsibilities and making a living), these other aims of education are corollaries, and essential but secondary aims.

Parenthetically it must be observed that education in the broad sense of the word continues during the entire lifetime of every one of us. The school system is only a partial and inchoate agency with respect to this task. Moreover, because it deals essentially with that which can be taught, it refers to the education and formation of intelligence more than of the will.

To help a child of man to attain his full formation as a man: if man were that kind of queer animal capable of science and with no spirit, which is fancied by most contemporary philosophers—a bee, a beaver, or a wolf having conversations and making atom bombs—education should be concerned with training him in specialized skills, symbolic logic, and adjustment to the environment. But if man is a fleshly creature endowed with spiritual intelligence—a person called to exercise and conquer freedom—education has to train him in the *humanities*—but what does this word humanities mean? Does it mean composing Latin verses, sitting down in a cozy study lined with bookshelves to read Epictetus and Montaigne, or airing opinions on who was the author of Shakespeare's plays and what was the date of the first edition of Proust's novels? That's a pleasant ideal, but reserved, I fear, for old professors in the short stories of young novelists.

I submit that the humanities are those disciplines which make man more human, or nurture in man his nature as specifically human, because they convey to him the spiritual fruit and achievements of the labor of generations, and deal with things which are worth being known for their own sake, for the sake of truth or the sake of beauty. Such things bring to us, in one way or another, the impact of the transcendentals, and oblige us to think *really*, or at the level of universality. They make us aware of the "great moral, aesthetic and religious principles" which "have created our culture" and which are, as Professor Whitney J. Oates puts it, "truth, freedom, integrity, beauty, courage, justice, love and humility."[1] Knowledge of these things helps man to advance toward liberty, fosters in him civilized life, and is by nature in tune with the mind's natural aspiration to wisdom.

Such is, I think, the genuine notion of the humanities that we must keep in mind. The same notion, moreover, applies to the liberal arts—that is, to those intellectual disciplines which not only, as the ancients saw it, fit the condition of free man in opposition to servile activities, but which,

[1] *Princeton Alumni Weekly*, May 9, 1952, p. 11.

more profoundly, equip man to become actually free in his mind and judgment, as well as in his internal mastery of the pressures of his environment, of fate or misfortune, and of himself and his own deficiencies.

Given this general notion, it is not surprising that arts and letters should play a major part in the humanities. For it is when things have been brooded over and elaborated in human minds, when nature and reality have passed through series and series of births and rebirths and lived an age-long life in the creative activity of the human spirit, that they are best prepared to feed and to challenge the spiritual powers of man. Great poets and thinkers are the foster-fathers of intelligence. Cut off from them, we are simply barbarous.

At this point we must insist on the special privilege that, in however changing forms, classical literature, especially Greek and Latin literature, will always have in the humanities, I mean for Western peoples. On the one hand, Greek and Latin authors belong to a past world, and thus, precisely because this world of theirs is for us a separated world, they appear to us in a state of isolation from our daily concerns, in a state, so to speak, of illusory eternity, which is most appropriate for the essential disinterestedness of authentically formative and liberating knowledge. And on the other hand, separated as the world in which they belong may be, they themselves take us to the very roots of our culture and civilization, to our own roots. The art and poetry of India or China, and their philosophies, bring to us splendid treasures and also belong in the humanities. But they cannot have in the humanities and in education the same privileged place as our Greek and Latin heritage has, they are not part of our blood. The art and poetry of modern times, and their philosophies, are also, of course, an integral part of the humanities, and they are closer than Greek and Latin literature to the interests of our heart and the delights of our intellect.

But they are fruits, not roots. No man is really educated who is in ignorance of his roots.

Finally, our culture is also inseparable from Hebrew tradition and the Scriptures. But Hebrew tradition and the Scriptures have to do with much more than Western culture; they have to do with the Kingdom of God. And so it is mainly through religion, and the Christian Church's own heritage, that they have had an essential impact on Western civilization. Consequently they should have their part—a crucial part—in education and the humanities, but less at the level of school education than at the level of religious life and inspiration (let us think of the role played by the liturgy, nourished as it is by the prophets and the psalms, in the education of Catholic peoples, or by the reading of the Bible in that of Protestant peoples). At the level of school education the rational, strictly human character of the Greek and Latin tradition is but a reason more for its privileged place in the humanities and the liberal arts.

The remarks I have just made have value as general principles; and general principles apply in the course of time in varied, analogical ways. We should never confuse a general principle with the particular way in which it was or is enforced in a given period of history. Now, with respect to the manner in which the humanities and education were conceived in past centuries, three observations seem to be necessary.

First: The matters which composed the heritage of culture and knowledge were of the highest quality and offered inexhaustible riches to the searching effort of the human mind. But they were comparatively small in extent and quantity and thus it was possible for a man not only to be genuinely cultivated in all of them but also to master creatively a variety of them, so as to attain the very level of intellectual virtues in his approach to universal knowledge.

Second: The humanities and liberal education were the

privilege of a few people, the youth of the ruling classes. The concept of man, as to practical and social application, was itself, to tell the truth, unconsciously restricted. The only people in whom the concept of man had succeeded in displaying its full implications were in antiquity those men who enjoyed the condition of free men, in contrast to slaves; later on, and over a long period, they were admittedly, as a matter of fact, those men who enjoyed possibilities for leisure, and guiding responsibility with respect to the mass—say, noblemen or gentlemen, or members of the third estate, or, after the Industrial Revolution, members of the upper bourgeoisie, in contrast to tradesmen and manual workers. Humanity, for all practical purposes, was represented by them. *Humanum paucis vivit genus.* The human race lives in a few, and for a few: this motto was a matter of common consent from Ancient Greece and Aristotle on to the advent of a better realization of the Christian message's temporal implications.

The requirements involved in the very concept of human nature with regard to education, I mean the need of man for the humanities and liberal education, were satisfied, accordingly, by the very fact that the children of the ruling classes were given this kind of education. The admirable effort started in the seventeenth century, especially with St. Jean-Baptiste de la Salle, toward popular education was intended to instruct the children of the people in those grace-given humanities which are Christian truths and Christian virtues, but apart from that, to train them only in the three R's and in practical and utilitarian, vocational and technical disciplines. The very idea of liberal education for them was made inconceivable by the social conditions.

Furthermore, the aristocratic or restricted liberal education of which we are speaking was dominated by the philosophical notion of man which reigned in the past three centuries. This notion, Cartesian in its origin, remained fundamentally rationalistic, even when the influence of British philosophy and the French enlightenment made it veer toward empiricism. We have here, I think, one of the reasons for the rationalistic bias with which liberal education was so long imbued, and for the prevalence of a merely theoretical and abstract formation, in accordance with a spurious speculative ideal, more Epicurean than Aristotelian, according to which the enviable condition of the man of leisure was to sit down before the spectacle of the achievements of the human mind and to enjoy the pleasure of "general ideas" without engaging in the reality of things either his heart or his intellect itself.

My third observation is that the humanities and liberal education aim, as I have said, to provide man with what makes him more truly man—disinterested knowledge, understanding, untrammeled ability to think; more particular ends and applications are but corollaries. Yet, among these more particular ends and applications, the most important one is that which deals with the life and common good of political society. Let us say, then, that in past centuries the principal and most essential among the secondary ends of liberal education was the preparation of youth (the youth of the upper classes) for ruling or governing responsibilities.

Our epoch presents quite opposite characteristics.

First: Whatever shortcomings or parasitical errors may have impaired democracy, at least a progress of crucial import has been brought about by democratic thought: any discord has been abolished, in the idea of man, between the metaphysical and the social extent of this idea, between the recognition of an individual as a human being endowed with a certain nature in the cosmos and his recognition as a human being endowed with certain rights in society. All men have in the social body a right to the possibility of achieving, each one in his own way, a condition of life appropriate to the requirements of human nature, or to the opportunity of attaining the stature of man, first of all as to his own inner and spiritual development. This is, at least, the basic tenet and immutable ideal, however remote from its attainment the world may still be. As a result, the notion of education restricted to a few has lost any possible justification, and is, in actual fact, progressively fading away. Education in the authentically human sense of the word, liberal education, can no longer be the privilege of a few. It must henceforth be made available to all—to the very extent to which human societies are civilized societies, and in the very measure in which democratic civilization is to survive.

Second: There is or should be no longer, in democratic societies, any class endowed with the special function of ruling or governing, be it a class hereditarily constituted through the power of wealth, or politically established through the power of a totalitarian party. Government is government of the people, by the people, and for the people, through representatives whose authority to govern is a participation in the authority of the people. Consequently, the principal and most essential among the secondary aims of education must be the preparation of youth (all youth) for active citizenship and political understanding of the common good.

Third: We are farther from our historical roots than the classical centuries were. An immense development of new knowledge has taken place. Science has opened everywhere new ways of research and discovery which require a more and more specialized approach—not to speak of philosophy which has been broken into conflicting pieces by its subservience to science, and has, at the same time, preyed upon science with its own interpretations of scientific results. The Scientific Revolution has had as large an impact on the mind as the Industrial Revolution on society. Thus the matters with which education has to deal, the matters which compose our heritage of culture and knowledge, have immensely increased in extent and quantity. Universal knowledge remains the ideal goal of education; but no man can henceforth, in his approach to universal knowledge, hope to develop the various intellectual virtues and intellectual skills necessary to master creatively its various fields.

On the other hand, old Cartesian rationalism has given way to opposite philosophical trends, which are no better, since they are mainly empiricist or positivist, but which at least have brought to an end the merely theoretical, abstract and angelistic bias of traditional education. Thus it is that a kind of synthesis and integration, along Aristotelian lines, has become now possible, in which the superior importance of the awakening of thought to disinterested knowledge would be maintained, but the real psychology of the child would be taken into consideration, and the essential part played by the senses and sense-training in education, especially as to its means and methods, would be recognized.

CONTEMPORARY EDUCATION AND THE HUMANITIES

All the previous considerations oblige us to become aware of two problems which are, in my opinion, of capital importance for the evolution of education in our modern age. I should like to go thoroughly into both of them. The first problem deals with the very notion of the humanities and liberal arts. We have, I think, to work out a more comprehensive concept of the humanities, and to recast and enlarge a great deal the list of liberal arts.

I insisted at the beginning on the pre-eminent value of arts and letters, and especially of Greek and Latin literature, in liberal education. I still cling to these principles. But I assume that the conditions of our times call for a new way of realization. On the one hand I would suppress from training in the humanities (I mean during the high-school and college years) the teaching of dead languages: first, because the burden of knowledge to be acquired by youth is too great to permit the many hours of study which are demanded by such teaching if it has a minimum of seriousness; second, because there is no good in useless boredom, and the teaching of Greek and Latin would chiefly represent a waste of time for the great many destined to forget them. Greek and Latin authors should be more than ever at the core of humanistic disciplines. But better to read them carefully in translation than to learn their language and to read only bits of their works in textbooks; Greek and Latin (and possibly Hebrew) should be learned later on—much more rapidly and fruitfully—but only by graduate students specializing in languages, literature, history, or philosophy.

On the other hand the outstanding value of modern literature and poetry—and not only of national but of world literature—for humanistic education and knowledge of man should be greatly emphasized, and similarly the value of the fine arts. But we would have also to realize that the humanistic disciplines must henceforth comprise—according to an integral appreciation of what is of a nature to make man more aware of his own humanity—appropriate knowledge in anthropology and the history of cultures and civilizations, physics and the history of sciences, even technology (from the point of view of the creative activity of the spirit) and the history of manual work and the mechanical arts. Such knowledge is inherent in the genuine notion of the humanities, as I have tried to elucidate it in the first part of this lecture.

At this point we are confronted with the question of the liberal arts. I discussed this question some years ago in a book on education,[2] but now I would like to carry my discussion further and make my conclusions more complete.

The medieval notion of the seven liberal arts derived from the Hellenistic notion (whose limits were, besides, more or less vague) of "general training"; the medieval seven arts, thus inherited from the school tradition of late antiquity,

[2] See *Education at the Crossroads*, Part III.

were constituted on the one hand by the three literary arts
of the Carolingian Trivium—grammar, rhetoric, and dialectic—and, on the other hand, by the four mathematical
disciplines of the Quadrivium—geometry, arithmetic, astronomy, and musical theory—a division which was traditional from the time of Archytas of Tarentum, if not of
Pythagoras himself. Now it is clear that whereas the concept itself of liberal art has intrinsic permanent value, such
an arrangement of the liberal arts depended for a great
part on historical contingencies; and that the listing of liberal arts must conform, in each epoch, with the extent and
degree of humanistic knowledge then actually possessed.

Given the scientific development characteristic of our
times, I therefore submit that the most appropriate listing
might seem somewhat as follows:

In a preliminary division, which I should like to call the
Pre-Liberal Arts, we would place these matters, the knowledge of which concerns the intellectual instruments and
logical discipline required for the ventures of reason, as well
as the treasure of factual and experiential information
which must be gathered in the memory. Thus we would have,
on the one hand, grammar, with a view to comparative
grammar and linguistics, logic and languages, and, on the
other hand, history, national history and the history of the
civilized world, with connected subjects such as geography.

Coming now to the liberal arts themselves, or to those
matters the knowledge of which refers directly to the creative or perceptive activity of the intellect and to its thirst
for seeing and understanding, we would have in the first
place a trivium, concerned with the creative activity of the
mind, and beauty to be perceived and delighted in. This
trivium would comprise, first, the art of thought-expression
or creative expression—let us say, to pay a tribute to Calliope,
the first Muse and the mother of Orpheus, eloquence, an art
which gives the mind respect for words and a sense of the
dignity and accuracy of thought, and the disregard of which

is so harmful to modern man; secondly, literature and poetry; and thirdly, art, that is to say the fine arts, but also mechanical arts and technology, the study of which pertains to liberal and humanistic disciplines, to the extent to which it is made in a philosophical and historical light, and from the point of view of the creative energies of the human spirit.

And in the second place we would have a quadrivium, concerned with the knowing and rational activity itself, the intuitive and judicative activity of the mind—truth to be perceived and assented to "according to the worth of evidence." This quadrivium would comprise, first, mathematics and the history of mathematics; second, physics and the natural sciences, and their history; third, the human sciences—that is, in particular, anthropology and the history of cultures and civilization; and fourth, philosophy, that is, on the one hand, philosophy of nature, philosophical psychology, metaphysics and the theory of knowledge (with connected subjects such as experimental psychology), and, on the other hand, ethics and political and social philosophy, with connected subjects such as sociology.[3]

LIBERAL EDUCATION AND DEMOCRACY

Let us pass now to the second basic problem, or set of problems, with which education in present and future times is and will be confronted. These problems arise from the very tenet, *liberal education for all,* which must guide education in a real democracy. How can liberal education be deprived of the aristocratic or oligarchic character it possessed for so many centuries? How is it possible to extend liberal education, and training in the humanities, not to a few, more or less destined to a life of leisure, but to all, destined as they

[3] For a further discussion of the role of physics and of the natural and human sciences in liberal education, see pp. 69–71.

are to be involved in the toils and anxieties of daily labor and the hard necessity of making a living, and who need, for this, vocational and technical training?

Here I should like to observe that a life of leisure, even for a few, is decidedly something of the past. Work, in some form or other, is becoming a universal law. On the other hand, while all are called to work in the human society, the technical equipment of our industrial civilization will progressively provide all, as a rule, with an increasing possibility for leisure, and permit all youth to pursue their studies until the age which corresponds to the end of college years. I should like also to observe that the very recasting of the list of liberal arts, and broadening of the humanities, of which I spoke a moment ago, would result in making access to liberal education easier for all, since liberal education would cease being considered an almost exclusively literary education. As a matter of fact, liberal education ceased long since being an almost exclusively literary education; yet this occurred in a merely empirical—and detrimental—manner, as a kind of admitted betrayal of liberal education, because one continued at the same time to think of it in terms of the old pattern. On the other hand the theorists of the progressive school were to renounce liberal education under the pretext that it did not answer the needs of our times. Well, what we have to do is rather to integrate these needs in the renewed concept of a genuine liberal education.

But the main point I should like to make now does not deal with the *broadening* of the matters comprised within the scope of the liberal arts and the humanities. It deals with a *restriction* of the burden imposed on the student and of the curriculum, as concerns the very ways and perspective in which the matters in question have to be taught. What seems to me to be the most essential requirement of sound educational theory appropriate to our times is to bring out and enforce the concept of basic *liberal education* (during the entire period of formation of the adolescent, till the end of college).

I attach crucial importance to this concept, which I shall try to elucidate in a moment. Let me say that during the period in question, from the beginning of high school to the end of college, education cannot be liberal if it is not *basic* liberal education. And let me start from a factual observation: there are two opposite extremes which the educational system has great difficulty avoiding; when it realizes that one is not good, it shifts toward the other, but both of them are bad. On the one hand the young person is imagined as a reduction of the adult, a small adult to be crammed with adult science; then one believes that the entire universe of knowledge which no individual adult can master, but which has been prepared for the collective body of adult culture by the collective effort of generations, and which is in the state of *science*, must be inculcated in the young person in a diminutive form, by means of pills or tablets supposedly containing all this science at high concentration. Let us call this concept the concept of education as *encyclopedic inculcation*. Of course neither can science remain science while being diminished, nor can the young person really assimilate pills or tablets of concentrated science. As a result of such a process of encyclopedic inculcation, we would have only a reduced simulacrum of adult science in the young person, and he would be, at best, a learned intellectual dwarf.

On the other hand—this is the opposite extreme—the child and the youth are imagined as a particular species the very essence of which is divided from that of the adult; then one believes that the mental universe peculiar to this species, which is a universe of ignorance, must be served, assisted and stimulated in its free development, in taking care not to interfere by means of any articulate communication of what has been acquired by adult knowledge or by any discipline formative of the intellect. Let us call this concept the concept of education as nursery accommodation. Of course no spontaneous transformation of the state of savagery into the state of civilization in the course of individual evolution—

and, as regards the school, no chaotic exchange of opinions between teachers and pupils, aiming at a painless titillation of the minds of the latter, and accompanied by a lot of factual information—can really prepare the youth to become a man. As a result of such a process of nursery accommodation, we would have only a formless mind, and the youth would become, at best, a good-humored childish adult.

To the extent to which they favor the first of these two opposite extremes, educators confuse the real formation of intelligence, and the awakening to integrated thought and knowledge, with indoctrination of adult science in the young person. And thus they warp the primary aim of education, especially liberal education.

To the extent to which they favor the second of these two opposite extremes, educators simply give up any real formation of intelligence and any awakening to integrated thought and knowledge, and thus they forsake the primary aim of education, especially liberal education.

If we are to avoid both of these opposite extremes in a definite, clearly oriented, and philosophically grounded manner, we have to understand the far-reaching significance and the practical import of the distinction, which we made in the preceding essay, between *natural intelligence* and *intellectual virtues*.[4] Basic liberal education is directed to the natural intelligence of youth. It deals with universal knowledge on a non-scientific level and does not attempt to go beyond it into the area proper to the intellectual virtues.

Any educational task is regulated by a more or less conscious image or idea of the kind of adult man that the youth should become. What should this directive image or idea be? As we have already said, basic liberal education does not regard students as future professors or specialists, nor as future gentlemen or members of a privileged class, but as future citizens who must act as free men capable of making sound

4 See pp. 13–15.

and independent judgments and of enjoying the common heritage of knowledge and beauty. This gives us some criterion about the kind of learning such an ideal for adult age entails for youth.

Let me stress once again at this point that the objective of basic liberal education is not the acquisition of science itself or art itself, and of the intellectual virtues involved, but rather the grasp of their *meaning* and the comprehension of the truth and beauty they yield, a grasp of which natural intelligence is capable and for which it thirsts. We grasp the *meaning* of a science or art when we understand its object, nature, and scope, and the particular species of truth and beauty it discloses to us. The objective of basic liberal education is to see to it that the young person grasps this truth or beauty through the natural powers and gifts of his mind and the natural intuitive energy of his reason backed up by his whole sensuous, imaginative, and emotional dynamism. Imagination, in actual fact, plays here as important a part as reason. As for the content of knowledge, this must be determined by the requirements of the grasp in question. The guiding principle in this would be: less factual information and more intellectual enjoyment.

In point of fact, great progress has been made, I think, in the adjustment, of which I am speaking, of education to natural intelligence. The achievements of modern education in this regard are highly valuable. But sometimes it was less a question of adjustment to natural intelligence than to natural inertia, and reluctance to exert intellectual effort. And in another respect the present educational system falls short of genuine liberal education and suffers, as a rule, from a crucial lack: namely, the lack of unity and integration. There is no universality without unity. A universal knowledge which is not unified and integrated according to a firmly recognized hierarchy of values is not universal knowledge, but scattered and chaotic knowledge. Unity and integration are an essential need of natural intelligence. Lacking them, no teaching can really respect the dignity and integrity of natural intelligence, and that power of intuitive grasping which is its genuine and living fire, infinitely more precious than all instrumental or mechanical operations which might be performed just as well by electronic brains; lacking unity and integration, no teaching can be done in such a way that the mind of the student remains always master of the matter offered to it (which is a primary rule of education), and no teaching can contribute to making the student finally prepared and equipped to think, in the true sense of this word, as a free and responsible human person—which is the kind of perfection of which natural intelligence is capable, even though it is not yet perfected by intellectual virtues, and to which basic liberal education must essentially tend.

In view of the preceding remarks, the distinction between basic liberal education and higher learning or graduate studies should be emphasized, for basic liberal education is concerned with the knowledge appropriate to natural intelligence, and graduate studies with the knowledge appropriate to the intellectual virtues.

Basic liberal education would take in both high school and college. What I have called the pre-liberal arts would be taught during the high-school years, with the manner of teaching adapted to the freshness and spontaneous curiosity of budding reason, stirred and nourished by the life of the imagination.

During the college years basic liberal education in its final stages would be provided, and also the preparation for a particular field of activity. In my opinion, the best arrangement for this purpose would be to have the college divided into a number of Institutes,[5] all of which would be dedicated to basic liberal education, but each of which would deal with the preparatory study for a particular field of activity.

All of the students would be required to attend the courses

[5] See pp. 72–74.

in basic liberal education, but the number of hours devoted to certain of these courses would be different for the students in the various Institutes. And special courses would be offered in each Institute to enlighten the students on the vital relationship between the particular discipline he is taught and the chief disciplines of the common curriculum. In this way the proper hierarchy of values inherent in liberal education would be preserved, and the students would be offered the type of pre-professional training which, instead of impairing liberal education, would make them more vitally interested in it and more deeply influenced by it.

Since Tom is to exercise later a function in the social community as a farmer and John as a mathematician, and since both have to continue their education and develop their best potentialities as men in the course of their entire life, it is but normal that their special preparatory training should be integrated at an early stage in a general training in the humanities fit to quicken their entire life and given unquestioned primacy during college. On the one hand, special preparatory training is necessary—all the more so as the greatest achievements of man are often attained when he is still young; on the other hand, general training in the humanities, and trained capacities to think as a responsible person, whose reason is free from subservience to instinct and passion, group reflexes, prejudices or interests, are the primary need and obligation of man *qua* man; and they are, moreover, a pre-required condition not only for genuine citizenship, but also for inventive and progressive activity in the most practical or specialized matters.

The notion of basic liberal education, with the kind of recasting of the list of liberal arts and the method of teaching the humanities we have considered, is of a nature, it seems to me, to give practical and existential value to the concept of *liberal education for all*,[6] for it is adapted to all the real

[6] This notion of *liberal education for all* is treated further on pp. 69–75. The question of the conflicting interests of brighter and duller students is often raised when *liberal education for all* is discussed. For Professor Maritain's views on this question see pp. 148–49 (Editors' Note).

needs which the liberal education of the past was reproached with not being able to satisfy.

EDUCATION AND THE PRESENT CRISIS

To conclude this lecture, I should like to observe that the task of education is growing rapidly, not only in importance but also in difficulty, in a world which, at least for the time being, is becoming, I would say, to a large extent existentialist and irrational.

I have used the word "existentialist" because the existentialist philosophies of today are but passing mirrors of the time. It is our world which is growing weary of reason and ideas—it keeps on using them because it cannot do without them, but only in order to make them tools for advertising techniques, and for any kind of sham justification for reliance on the elementary fears, reflexes, and competitions of bare existence.

Education is essentially education in the humanities and in the genuine ability to think. And it has to perform its task in a world which thirsts, no doubt, for the liberation of the human person, but in which powerful trends tend to make the human person and the human mind controlled by the constraints of matter, and thought controlled by action.

As Allen Tate puts it, "It is a tragedy of contemporary society that so much of democratic social theory reaches us in the language of 'drive,' 'stimulus' and 'response.' This is not the language of freedom, it is the language of slaves. The language of freemen substitutes for these words, respectively, *end, choice* and *discrimination.*" "The general intelligence," Allen Tate goes on to say, "must not be committed to the illiberal specializations that the nineteenth century has proliferated into the modern world: specializations in which means are divorced from ends, action from sensibility, matter from mind, society from the individual, religion from moral agency, love from lust, poetry from thought, communion from experience, and mankind in the community from men in the crowd. There is literally no end to this list of dissociations because there is no end, yet in sight, to the fragmenting of the western world."[7] It is in a world subject to this process of fragmenting, and which dreams of having every man pigeonholed for a specialized task in a technocratic beehive, that education has to pursue its work of unification and integration. It is in a world subjected to a process of perversion of the function of language that education has to prepare the young person to respect the meaning and properties of words.

Education is education for freedom. And the world within which it has to fulfill its duties is sick with a frustrated longing for freedom and beauty, and has unlearned the primary conditions and requirements of freedom.

A striking sign of the practical materialism which threatens the roots of freedom today is our current notion of work as supreme end and of leisure as sheer relaxation. Work is good in itself; it is the normal condition of man. But work is not the end and perfection of human life. Work is essentially a means—toward an end which is the free activity, perfecting man in his innermost life, of communion with truth and beauty, and of the gift of oneself in love. Such free and immanent activity presupposes work, of course; it can inspire work and superabound in it. But of itself it is leisure activity, requiring that *free time* where man can be within himself and listen to God within himself. It has its peak in the grace-given contemplation and love of those heroes in spiritual life who are the saints. But it is available to all in its lower degrees, through the fruits of knowledge, art and poetry—of the humanities—that are conveyed in the common heritage of mankind, and through that other kind of fruit which is self-sacrifice in devotion to those one loves.

[7] Allen Tate, "The Man of Letters in the Modern World," *Collected Essays* (Denver: Alan Swallow, 1959), pp. 388–90. (The Phi Beta Kappa Address, University of Minnesota, May, 1952.)

"Nobody," Thomas Aquinas has said, "can live without delectation. That is why he who is deprived of spiritual delectations goes over to the carnal."[8] Neither can freedom live without spiritual delectations.

As long as our world makes work the end of human life, and consequently confuses genuine leisure and its free activities with animal relaxation, hypnotic pleasure or amusement which has no value except as it has fun instead of spiritual delectation, as long as it claims to cultivate the mind but simply ignores the soul, it will foster serfdom, not freedom, and thwart with its own general behavior the effort of education toward liberation of the mind and toward helping man to become man.

The trends I have just pointed out are neither definitive nor insuperable. Freedom and the spirit may be threatened; it depends on them to hold the threat in check.

I do not submit my remarks on the present crisis of our world for the sake of pessimism or melancholy. I submit them to stress the fact that the task of education and educators is all the greater and all the more necessary as it has to be carried on against the general stream, and to insist that the cause of the humanities does not depend on the school system alone, but also and first of all on a reformation of our world. The world will never be wise. At least it can be aware that it needs wisdom, and believe in the true scale of values, and yearn for wisdom as the highest virtue of the human mind and to know reality and to guide life. As to education, its final aim is to prepare men for wisdom. "The end of liberal education is wisdom," as President Harold Dodds of Princeton University insisted in a recent address. And as to the humanities, they are in jeopardy if they do not tend to wisdom, just as human wisdom is in jeopardy if it does not tend to a higher wisdom, that God gives in love, and which alone can truly set man free.

[8] *Summa Theol.*, II–II, q. 35, a. 4, *ad secundum.*

Chapter Four

MORAL AND SPIRITUAL VALUES IN EDUCATION

EDUCATION AND THE MORAL VIRTUES

Ever since the time of Socrates and Plato the problem "Can ethical behavior be taught?" and "How to teach ethical behavior" has been the ordeal of teachers. Socrates and Plato believed that virtue is knowledge; Aristotle answered that knowledge is of little avail for virtue and that virtue is not a matter of teaching. And this is quite true, on the whole.

Hence the paradox of schools, colleges and universities: they have to help young people to become men and women worthy of the name; now, what is most important in relation to such a goal, if not right moral conduct? Yes, but right moral conduct is not a matter of teaching. Then, must we say that the educational system should not be concerned at all with moral education and should leave to other and more fundamental agencies, namely, the family and the churches, all the responsibility for preparing the same pupils to act and behave in the right way, according to the demands of justice and love?

Such an answer would be in tune neither with truth nor with the spirit of this country. American education, in actual fact, has always stressed with good reason the moral task which devolves upon the school system—though now and then, let me say, some theorists in education put the emphasis a little too much on good citizenship and well-adjusted social behavior, and a little insufficiently on justice and love and on integrated knowledge as well—while some other theorists, like G. Stanley Hall, thought that the instincts of the child should be given free rein, in order for him naturally to pass from the stage of savagery to the civilized stage.

At this point, and as a preface to our discussion, it is relevant, I believe, to lay stress on two basic assertions which have been recognized for centuries. In the first place: the direct and primary responsibility of the school is not moral, but intellectual in nature—namely, responsibility for the normal growth of the intellect of the students, the acquisition by them of articulate and sufficiently universal knowledge and the development of their own inner intellectual capacities. The school has primarily to teach them how to think.

In the second place: the responsibility for moral education rests directly and primarily on the family on the one hand and on the other hand on the religious community to which the family of the young person belongs. I would like to add, parenthetically, that for the student of human civilizations it is clear that morality in mankind is inherently tied up with religion and faith. Of course, there can be "good pagans," and "good atheists." Yet—and as far as the deep-seated opinions which sometimes escape consciousness are concerned— one may wonder whether these good pagans and good atheists are not in actual fact pseudo-pagans and pseudo-atheists rather than real pagans and real atheists. In any case, from the point of view of the intellect, there is no primary and unshakable foundation for the unconditional character of moral law and moral obligation, except God. So it is that, as was said in the *Regents' Statement on Moral and Spiritual Training in the Schools,* "Belief in and dependence upon Almighty God was the very cornerstone upon which our Founding Fathers builded."[1] As a result, it appears that

[1] Statement issued by the Board of Regents of the University of the State of New York.

the facilities offered by the school system for the religious training of pupils (outside the school premises, in the case of state-controlled schools) are an imperative requirement of the common good.

But enough of this parenthesis. Now the point I would like to insist upon is that, if the first responsibility of the school deals with the intellect and with knowledge, and if the first and direct responsibility for moral education belongs to the family group and the churches, nevertheless the responsibility of the educational system in this regard is, however indirect, no less necessary. I said a moment ago that, according to Aristotle, knowledge is of little avail for virtue. Aristotle's statement is true in this sense, that to know what courage or self-control is is not enough to act courageously or exercise self-control. But knowledge is a general precondition necessary for virtue, a general precondition necessary for decent, generous and upright moral behavior, in this sense that no right human life can have solidity, stability and duration without a vision of the world in which firm convictions about moral and spiritual values appears rationally founded and the validity of the old Platonic maxim, "It is better to suffer injustice than to inflict it," is clearly seen.

Now—and by the very fact that school and college education must teach students how to think truly and comprehensively—is it not the job of school and college education to develop such a vision of the world and such firm convictions about moral and spiritual values—in other words, such an integrated knowledge destined to grow into real wisdom? Thus it is that, though school and college education has essentially to do with the intellect and with knowledge, it exercises at the same time an indirect, but crucial impact on the health of the will and has a basic moral task to perform. This task—which deals with the intellectual foundations of moral life and with the development of the sense of those realities which are spiritual in nature, like truth and beauty

—this moral task of education is growing today, it seems to me, more and more important, as mankind is confronted with materialist or positivist philosophies which make moral standards completely relativized, and with the "other-directed" or sheeplike cast of mind which our industrial and technological civilization tends to develop. If such a cast of mind, for which the only essential thing is adjustment to environment, were to take the upper hand, human morality would come down, for example, to conscientiously choosing as an ethical standard the average behavior described in the Kinsey Report, and we would forget that there can be no society of freemen without the ferment of personal consciences which do not adjust to environment, but resist environment and prefer to obey the law of God rather than the law of men.

THE FOSTERING OF MORAL AND SPIRITUAL IDEALS

In connection with the preceding considerations I would like to submit a few remarks.

In the first place I would like to insist that the development of the sense of spiritual realities and spiritual values, and that effort toward integrated knowledge and wisdom, which are usually associated with the notion of the humanities, are not the privilege of a category of discipline as against the others. To my mind, genuine humanities and genuine liberal arts embrace not only mathematics but physics and all natural sciences, and what is called today human sciences, and even technology, as well as literature, fine arts, history and philosophy. For the only thing which really matters here is the universal inspiration which permeates the teaching.

The great question, I believe, is to focus the teaching, in high schools and in college, on the creativity of the human mind, and the boundless resilience of its spiritual power; it is to make the students as fully aware as possible of this creativity, to which no electronic brain can ever reach, and of the steady effort through which mankind advances in its quest for knowledge, in the conquest of material nature and in the variegated manifestation of the potentialities hidden in man.

From this point of view it appears necessary, to be sure, to know the results of the works of the mind, but still more important to know the ways through which these results were achieved and the ceaseless process of discovery went on. Such an approach may apply to all the matters of the curriculum; it reveals everywhere the supramaterial fecundity of the imagination and the intellect at work together. In such a perspective science and poetry are as one; humanity appears as a single being growing from generation to generation, thanks to the inner quickening spirit it has received from God; and we realize that becoming capable of a bit of genuine spiritual experience and cognitive or creative intuition matters more, for the education of a young person and for the common good, than memorizing the entire *Encyclopaedia Britannica* and all the textbooks of the world.

In the second place, I would like to observe that it would be poor psychology to believe that the mental atmosphere and the world of images in the midst of which the minds of children, and of adults as well, but especially of children, breathe and feed have no impact upon their moral development. So, for instance, it is clear, in my opinion, that those comics which appeal to the most vulgar animal instincts and nourish children with images of violence and brutality tend to make the level of common morality lower and lower.

Yet it is not on the negative aspect, it is on the positive aspect of the picture that I wish to insist: I mean to say, on that endeavor to offer to the children of man genuine images of grandeur and heroism which is, to my mind, one of the great tasks of education in the moral field.

The French philosopher Henri Bergson has shown, in his

book *The Two Sources of Morality and Religion*,[2] that mankind cannot do without what he calls the appeal of the hero
—the attraction exercised by the great figures who act on us
by their example, having led, in love and dedication, a life
superior to our ordinary lives. The need to have a moral ideal
embodied in a concrete human being who shows us the way
is one of the basic needs of our moral growth. It is normal
for a young person to feel enthusiasm for a hero or a saint of
his or her choice, and to cling to him and to dream of him
and try to imitate him. This hero, whom we love and who
draws us above ourselves, is for us a real master in moral life.

I believe that in providing children and young persons
with a moral atmosphere of grandeur and heroism the school
and the high school can accomplish a duty in which many
families are now failing. I am thinking of classes in which
teacher and students would study and discuss the lives of
the heroes of mankind—all those who have been heroically
dedicated to a great intellectual or human mission, in all
times and in all countries of the globe and in every domain
in which love and self-sacrifice can be at work. Here again
may I be permitted to refer to a pronouncement of the Regents? In their *Statement on America's Moral and Spiritual
Heritage*, they wrote: "Biography will keep before pupils
inspired examples of character and encourage them with
'the habitual vision of greatness.'"[3] At each grade such
teaching can easily be adapted to the mentality peculiar to
the age of the pupils. And I think it can arouse in them a
lively interest and can exert a salutary influence on them. Not
only would they have, thus, an opportunity to become personally acquainted with heroic examples, but they would
become aware of the immense effort of good will and generosity through which mankind and civilization have developed; and they would become familiar not only with the

[2] Chapter I, "Moral Obligation."
[3] Statement issued by the Board of Regents of the University of the State
of New York.

great figures of their own national history and with the moral
convictions and spiritual flame that animated them, but also
with the great figures and heroes of world history.

With my third remark I am afraid I may appear a con-
firmed old-fashioned European, yet this would be perhaps
no necessary proof that I am wrong. My contention is that
there are many excellent things in modern methods and so-
called progressive education, but that the idea of making
the school into a paradise of freedom, untrammeled happiness and doing as you please for children is no better for
their psychological and moral welfare than the old and ne-
farious idea of education by the rod. Modern psychology has
become aware of the fact that it is a basic need of the child
himself to feel both protected and guided by somebody invested with unquestionable authority—and this first of all
in the family, of course, but also in the school. The frustration of such a need leaves the child in a vacuum which invites
neurosis and anxiety; it is, to be sure, the worst of those frus-
trations which today's parents are so desperately eager to
avoid.

It is true that a teacher teaches a human subject, Tom or
Mary, and that his authority must always be intent on en-
couraging the child and appealing to his or her own power
of insight and understanding. But it is no less true that he
teaches an object—mathematics or grammar—and has primarily to make the human subject capable of freely and
eagerly submitting to the object and the requirements of the
object; he has to teach his pupils the exacting ways through
which they prepare for an adult life where they will be
obliged to make the best of situations *not* of their choosing
and to do not as they please but as they ought.

And I think that in making serious demands of this sort
upon young persons, the school develops the kind of climate
which is the most appropriate to foster, indirectly and in a
quite general way, those moral virtues which are not a

matter of teaching and which are rooted in the free initiative and effort of the human individual.

May I be permitted to make a final point—somewhat utopian perhaps—by way of conclusion?

The school is not only, according to its essential function, a place of teaching; it is also a kind of social community or small republic, in which students and teachers live and work together. From this point of view I am wondering whether—in order better to compensate for what is too often lacking in families with respect to moral education—it would not be desirable to make use of the good will of the best and most reliable pupils and to have them grouped in self-organized teams intent on improving the work and discipline of their own members, as well as their sense of fairness, justice and good fellowship in their mutual relations.

Such a collective responsibility might, I believe, develop in young persons genuine moral experience and the actual needs of some basic, elementary moral dispositions. The kinds of workshops in moral life constituted by the teams in question might not only make the common school discipline more alive, but also provide the students with more effective beginnings of a real formation of the will.

The value of self-organized teams of young people concerned with improving the behavior of the community has been tested with success in a certain number of particular cases. Yet I have no idea whether and how it might be put to work in public schools with large student populations. So it is only in a tentative way and as a quite humble suggestion, that I ventured today to outline this idea.

Chapter Five

MORAL EDUCATION

I do not pretend here to treat the question of Moral Education in a complete manner. I wish only to emphasize certain points that seem to me especially important from the philosophical angle.

There are four main points which I should like to discuss.

First: the nature and the limitations of the domain and function of the school with regard to moral education.

Second: the concrete, existential relationship between morality and religion.

Third: the basic role of the family in moral education.

Fourth: the moral teaching in the school.

THE ROLE OF THE SCHOOL IN MORAL EDUCATION

Before coming to my first point, I should like first of all to make it clear that a sharp distinction must be made between two essential parts of moral education, namely the *direct formation* of the will, or of the dynamism of human desires and freedom, and the *indirect moral formation* by means of the intellect's enlightenment. And the former depends basically not on the school and the university, but on the family —and on that spiritual family which is the Church.

At this point we may observe that in education broadly understood—I do not mean teaching—we may observe that educational training is in reality less an ethical art than a moral virtue implying a large part of art; it is in its very roots the practical wisdom (or, in Aristotelian terms, "prudence") of the head of the family. Because this particular ethical wisdom must necessarily involve a great deal of knowledge and a great deal of art and technical preparation as an essential ingredient, especially with regard to the intellectual formation of the child, it happened in antiquity that the father of the family shifted the responsibility of the art of teaching onto the *pedagogue,* who was a slave of the father of the family. From that time on, the pedagogue was to grow and develop in a singular manner, and to emancipate himself. Please do not believe I am suggesting that schools and colleges should be considered slaves of the *paterfamilias:* I mean that the historical development and freeing of the school, while assuming more and more importance, did not and could not annihilate the normal link which relates the school to the family, and that the part of the school in education concerns essentially knowledge and intellectual development.

The school and the university constitute an educational sphere of their own, which is autonomous both with regard to the family and to the state—there takes place here that great humanistic privilege which is academic liberties, but in which the educational rights of the family and the educational rights of the political community have to be respected, and in actual fact intertwine. The school is not an organ either of the family or of the civil community; its position is free, not subservient, yet subordinated to superior and more primordial rights: subordinated, I should like to say, to the family's rights as regards primarily morality, to the state's rights as regards primarily intellectual equipment.

Thus we understand the fact that in proportion as the child grows, the emphasis of this double subordination changes: the school, which at the beginning is more subordinated to the concerns of the family than to those of the political community, becomes finally, with university teaching, more subordinated to the concerns of the political community than to those of the family. Because the family refers primarily to man as a living being, to be born both to physical and to moral life, whereas the political community refers primarily to man as a rational being, therefore it is entitled to make special requirements with regard to the acquisition of knowledge, and to see to it that instruction be given to and received by all. I do not mean by making school and college education everywhere a part of the public services of the cities or the states; I mean by exerting control over it, and by helping or subsidizing privately endowed institutions. No doubt, the political community is interested too in the acquisition of moral virtues. But on the one hand it is here confronted with rights more fundamental than its own, namely, the rights of the family and those of the Church, which, by virtue of its mission spiritually to beget man for eternal life, possesses a full right to education—to be exercised in accordance with just civil laws. On the other hand, the very possibilities of the political community in matters of moral education are of no greater extent than those of the school, which has to do, by its very nature, with intellectual enlightenment more than with any direct formation of the will.

At this point I must stress the distinction between the will, practical reason, and speculative reason. Speculative reason deals with knowledge for the sake of knowledge alone; practical reason, with knowledge for the sake of action and good human conduct; the will, with action itself and human conduct itself. When I say that school and college education is primarily concerned with knowledge and intellectual enlightenment, I do in no wise mean that it is only concerned with speculative knowledge and speculative reason: on the contrary, I am convinced that our present school and college education is too much taken up by theoretical knowledge, and that the part of ethics and morality in it needs to be strongly developed and emphasized. What I mean is that this practical part does not essentially deal with the direct formation of the inner powers of desire and will, of conscience and freedom, but does essentially deal with the formation and enlightenment of practical reason: that is, with teaching about the nature and principles and the very science of morality, and with that immense part of human knowledge which bears on human manners and human conduct.

MORALITY AND RELIGION

My second point deals with the concrete, existential relationship between morality and religion. Here a preliminary remark must be made. I just spoke of practical reason and moral teaching. As concerns now the will itself and the moral virtues, as having to be acquired and exercised by the individual person, ethical knowledge is indeed indispensable, yet, as a matter of fact, far from sufficient. For it is a question of right applications to and right judgment on particular cases; practical reason itself depends on the rectitude of the will and on the decisive trend of our very freedom. The melancholy saying of Aristotle, contrasting with the Socratic doctrine that virtue is only knowledge, is to be recalled in this connection. "To know," he said, "does little or even nothing for virtue."[1]

What does a great deal for virtue is love: because the root hindrance to moral life is basic egoism, and the chief yearning of moral life; liberation from oneself; and only love, being the gift of oneself, is able to remove this hindrance and to

[1] *II Ethic*, Ch. 4, 1105b; cf. Saint Thomas Aquinas, *III Sent.*, dist. 35, ques. I, art. 3.9.2, a.s.

bring this yearning to fulfillment. But love is surrounded by our central egoism and in perpetual danger of becoming entangled in and recaptured by it, whether this egoism makes the ones we love a prey to our devouring self-love, or merges them in the ruthless self-love of the group, so as to exclude all other men from our love. Love does not regard ideas or abstractions or possibilities; love regards existing persons. God is the only Person whom human love can fly to and settle in, so as to embrace also all other persons and be freed from egotistic self-love. If a man actually loves another human being by that love which in some degree always consists in dying for the one loved, he actually loves God, and God first, at least in that manner in which all beings, even an atom or a grain of wheat, love God more than themselves. Yet the natural love of God cannot be stabilized in man so as to love God above everything in an efficacious fashion, and to love also all men, and in some manner all beings, unless it is perfected by love of charity.

At this point we may observe that a profound link exists between the sense of love and the sense of sin. For both love and sin are mysteries the meaning of which is definitely seizable only with reference to God, and both depend on those depths of human personality and human freedom where man feels responsible for himself and is able to dispose of himself or give himself for some eternal pledge and through some irrevocable decision. In his book on *The Bourgeois Man*, Werner Sombart insists that man, in the rationalistic-capitalistic age, has become deprived of the sense of Being and the sense of Love. He became deprived, too, of the sense of Sin. Truly, we lost at the same time the sense of these three basic realities. Now to recover them is a matter of emergency for civilization. The sense of Love, the sense of Sin, the sense of Being, will be recovered at the same time, for they are intrinsically connected with each other. Or, rather, if we consider not the order of time, but the order of natural priorities, and if we remember that normally the curve of human achievements starts in the reason and ends in the will, we should say that the first to be recovered is the sense of Being, which primarily depends on the dynamism of speculative reason, then the sense of Sin, which primarily depends on the dynamism of conscience and practical reason, and then the sense of Love, which primarily depends on the dynamism of the will and inner tendential powers.

The previous considerations enlighten the question of the relationship between morality and religion. The core of morality is human reason, insofar as reason is the proximate rule of human actions. The core of religion is divine love, that is,, indivisibly, love of God and brotherly love. Christianity fastens the moral to the supramoral—the moral order and the moral virtues to the theological order and the theological virtues, the greatest of which is charity. Christianity makes law appendant to love, and in this way it saves morality. For not only are reason and law, even the law of God, powerless to drag the heart of man to action if it is not quickened by love, but the very perfection of moral life and human life is suprahuman and supramoral, being perfection in love. We are wounded by sin indeed, and at the same time called upon to perfection, and there is no morality without striving toward self-perfection. If we aim at the moral ideal of the honest and sensible man, our average common behavior will drop down below morality. It will be lifted up to morality if the supramoral call and inspiration of the saints pass through our laborious and defective human life.

Thus we may understand the paradox that natural law exists, as the very basis of morality, and that nevertheless no effort of reason to establish among men a firm system of morality based only on natural law has ever been able to succeed; that moral philosophy is a fundamental and necessary requirement of culture and civilization, and that nevertheless moral philosophy is unable to ground good conduct of men if it is not backed up by faith. I am not pretending that a man who believes only in reason cannot have a genuine ethics of his own and a high standard of moral life. Nor am I pretending that a religious man cannot be morally perverted, or that religious men have always a standard of moral conduct worthy of their faith. That is nonsense! Religious men know they are sinners; but they also know that while staggering along we may climb the road to renascence and spiritualization. What I maintain is that with regard to the average behavior of mankind, morality without religion undermines morality, and is able to sustain human life for but a few generations.

MORAL EDUCATION AND THE FAMILY

In order to come to my third point, the basic role of the family in moral education, I should like to recall that nothing in human life is of greater importance than intuition and love, and neither intuition nor love is a matter of training or learning. Yet education must be primarily concerned with them. As for love, the question is above all to liberate the spiritual energies of the soul; those energies of goodness are badly repressed by the false realism and vulgarity of the wicked philosophy of life which is current today. Contrary to the precept of Descartes, who, in his provisory rules of Morals, decided to imitate the customs and doings of his fellow-men, we must first of all encourage personal conscience not to hesitate to disagree with collective behavior for the sake of truth, on the condition, of course, that it is certainly a question of truth. Such is the rule of the Gospel: "Do not ye after their works; for they say, and do not."[2] The first step to be taken by everyone who wishes to act morally, and to keep alive in himself the sources of love, is to make up his mind not to act according to the general customs and doings of his fellow-men.

Love, human love as well as divine love, is not a matter of

[2] *Matt.* XXIII, 3.

training or learning, for it is a gift; the love of God is a gift of nature and of grace: that is why it can be the first precept. How could we be commanded to put into action a power which we have not received or may not first receive? Charity, or that love of God is communion in friendship, is a grace-given virtue, and grows, like other virtues, by its own acts. There are no human methods or techniques of getting or developing charity, no more than any kind of love. There is nevertheless education in this matter: an education which is provided by trial and suffering, and which primarily consists in removing impediments and obstacles to love, and first of all sin, and in developing moral virtues.

The help of educators is obviously needed here. As is the case with that which concerns in general the direct formation of the will, the educational sphere involved is first of all the family. Is not family love the primary pattern of any love uniting a community of men? Is not fraternal love the very name of that neighborly love which is but one with the love of God? No matter what deficiencies the family group may present in certain particular cases; no matter what trouble and disintegration the economic and social conditions of our day have brought to family life, the nature cannot be changed. And it is an essential law of the nature of things both that the vitality and virtues of love develop first in the family and that moral and religious training is first at work in the family. Not only the examples of the parents, and the rules of conduct which they inculcate, and the religious habits and inspiration which they further, and the memories of their own lineage which they convey, in short the educational work which they directly perform, but also, in a more general way, the common experiences and common trials, efforts, sufferings and hopes, and the daily labor of family life, and the daily love which pushes forward in the midst of slaps and kisses, constitute the normal fabric where the feelings and the will as of the child are naturally shaped. The society made up by his parents, his brothers and sisters, is the primary human society and human environment in which, consciously and subconsciously, he becomes acquainted with love and from which he receives his ethical nourishment. Here both conflicts and harmonies have educational value; a boy who has experienced common life with his sisters, a girl who has done so with her brothers, have gained unawares invaluable and irreplaceable moral advance as regards the relationship between the sexes. Over and above all, family love and brotherly love create in the heart of the child that hidden recess of tenderness and repose the memory of which man so badly needs, and in which perhaps after years of bitterness, he will immerse himself anew each time a natural trend to goodness and peace awakens in him. Father's and mother's love is the natural fostering of the sources of love within the child. If they love God, the child will also know through them the very countenance of such a love, and never forget it.

I am aware that the examples of the parents are not always good, nor their educational work always well directed, nor their very love for their children always genuine, nor the life of the family group always heartening. We all know that the worst abuses and psychic deviations and unjust sufferings are possible in family life and education. French novelists, notably François Mauriac and Philippe Heriat, made clear what power of moral destruction a bourgeois family may display, and how the despotic love of some mothers may ruin the life of their sons. The history of the family, all through the centuries, is no prettier than any human history. What I maintain is that nature exists and nothing can get rid of nature. There are freaks in nature; then exceptional measures must be taken. But let us speak of what happens as a rule. Even at the most mediocre average level, nature at play in family life has its own spontaneous ways of compensating after a fashion for its own failures, its own spontaneous processes of self-regulation, which nothing can replace, and provides the child with a moral formation and an experience of mutual love, however deficient it may be, which nothing can replace. Many birds fall from the nest. It would be nonsense to undertake to destroy all the nests fairly well prepared by mother-birds, and to furnish the forests of the world with better-conditioned artificial nests, and improved cages.

It is not my purpose to speak now of the other educational sphere directly concerned with the moral shaping of man, namely the Church, acting by means of its teaching, precepts, sacraments, and liturgy, and its spiritual training and guidance, as well as by its manifold initiatives and undertakings, youth movements and organizations. Suffice it to say that here again we are confronted with the law of love proper to family, this time the very family of God, since grace causes men to be of the lineage of God, and, according to St. Paul, "fellow-citizens with the saints, and of the household of God."[3] To grow in the love of God, and, by the same token, of our fellow-men, is the serious business in this household. St. Paul also says: "He that loveth his neighbor hath fulfilled the law."[4] So that all the moral work by means of which Christianity endeavors to bring up the human person, is centered on the development, strengthening and purification of that brotherly love which actually enables us to become the neighbor of any man, by having pity on him and caring for his wounds.

As concerns finally the role of school and college education with regard to love as the very soul of moral life, two principles which I consider basically important find here a particular application. On the one hand, with regard to direct influence on the will, the role of the school amounts above all to that premoral training which depends not on teaching, but on humble policy, common life and discipline of the school: here the basic mood should be given in actual fact by constant attention to the requirements of the rules of

[3] *Eph.* II, 19.
[4] *Rom.* XIII, 8.

justice in the school-community, and to the requirements of sincere fellowship and brotherly love. On the other hand, with regard to the indirect action on the will *by means of intellectual* enlightenment, the role of school and college education is momentous indeed, insofar as teaching of true or false knowledge has efficacy to liberate or hamper the spiritual energy of love within the soul. For it is by the fallacies of pseudo-science and false philosophy of life that love trying to find its way amidst the jumbled world of passions and instincts is often withered and killed. Nowhere is the vigilance and genuine information of the intellect of greater practical import. All errors which make fun of goodness, all those practical sophistries which keep moving in our atmosphere, and avail themselves of cheap Darwinism, cheap Machiavellianism or so-called realism to make youth despair of the power of truth and love, should be thoroughly discussed and accurately criticized. The existence and power of evil should be frankly faced: and faced also the existence and power of God, which are greater. The true laws of being and of human existence, which are hidden to an empiricist gaze, but which reason and faith perceive, and which finally imply that evil is a bad payer and that love has the last word, should be contemplated without flinching and elucidated. A teaching which, not by empty idealistic words, but by dint of intellectual strength and exact disquisition of reality, inspires trust in goodness and generosity, is surely not enough to awaken the well-springs of love in the depths of human freedom, but it is efficacious to protect them, when they are present, and to set them free.

MORAL TEACHING IN THE SCHOOL

At this point we may consider more closely the question of moral teaching in the school and the college. I pointed out a moment ago that as regards the actual acquisition of moral virtues, ethical knowledge is indeed indispensable, yet far from being sufficient. It is equally fair to reverse the statement, and to say: ethical knowledge is indeed far from being sufficient, but it is indispensable.

To know, if it is a question of speculative knowledge, does little for virtue: the little it does, nevertheless, is beyond question, because, on the average, knowledge—I mean knowledge which deals with objects "of most worth"—cleans and pacifies the mind; moreover speculative knowledge establishes the metaphysical principles concerning nature and the world which are the foundations of the ethical principles concerning human freedom and conduct. And to know these ethical truths, that is to possess practical and moral knowledge, to have practical reason enlightened and sound, does a great deal for virtue. I mean on the average. Virtue is not a by-product of knowledge, but true moral knowledge is a condition for virtue. As Father Gerald B. Phelan has remarked, "Human conduct is of its very nature reasonable and enlightened conduct, else it is not truly human." Thus the moral sciences are at the core of any true humanism. The education of man, therefore, necessarily involves a careful and extensive moral teaching. And since teaching is the proper job of the school and the college, obviously moral teaching concerning both personal and civic morals must be an essential part of the curriculum. The absence or poverty of such teaching in formal education is a great misfortune. Filling this gap will probably be one of the chief concerns of the reformation needed by our time. Moral teaching should be pursued all through formal education.

The trouble starts with the question of the nature and content of this teaching. Many efforts have been made in the last century, especially in Europe, with hopes which proceeded from Kantian inspiration, to build in and for schools a morality of their own, disconnected from any religious creed and based on pure reason. The result was thoroughly disappointing. Sociologism and positivism were to nibble and consume the ethics of pure reason. Moreover, an ethics which, like that of Kant, ignores nature, good and the trend to happiness, and conceives of itself as merely law-giving by virtue of categorical imperatives, suffers from an incurable internal weakness.

There exists, nevertheless, a natural law. And there is a valid moral philosophy. Is it not possible to found on natural law and moral philosophy a consistent moral teaching in the school and the college? My answer is, yes and no. Natural law is unwritten and unsystematized law—too natural, so to speak, to become a subject of schoolteaching without losing its most human truth, inexpressible in the manner of a code. Moral philosophy is philosophy—too highly and delicately rationalized to become a subject of schoolteaching (except at the time when it is taught as philosophy) without losing its most valuable truth, which depends on all the principles and truths of philosophical reason. I would state, therefore, that in a good college curriculum moral philosophy should be taught—both through lectures and seminars—during the last two college years. But I think that during the years which precede philosophical training, no special teaching and courses should be given on morality abstractedly detached from its religious environment. Natural morality, however, natural law, and the great ethical ideas conveyed by civilization should be taught during these years. They are the very treasure of classical humanism; they must be communicated to the youth, not as a subject of special courses, but as embodied in the humanities and liberal arts, especially as an integral part of the teaching of literature, poetry, fine arts, and history. This teaching should be permeated with the feeling and concern of such values. The reading of Homer, Aeschylus, Sophocles, Herodotus, Thucydides, Demosthenes, Plutarch, Epictetus, Marcus Aurelius (better to read them carefully in translation than to learn their language and to read only bits), the reading of Virgil, Terence, Tacitus and Cicero, of Dante, Cervantes, Shakespeare,

Milton, Pascal, Racine, Montesquieu, Goethe, Dostoevski, feeds the mind with the sense and knowledge of natural virtues, honor, pity, of the dignity of man and of the spirit, the greatness of human destiny, the entanglements of good and evil, the *caritas humani generis,* more than any course in natural ethics. It conveys to the youth the moral experience of mankind.

So much for *natural morality.* Another point deals with morality as backed up by faith and involving supernatural life. I previously discussed the unbreakable relationship which, in actual existence, links morality with religion. Truth to tell, merely natural or rational ethics, if it is taken as a complete system of morality, is abstract ethics, dealing with a possible man, not with man in his concrete and real existential status. Ethics is able really to constitute a full practical science only on the condition that it be a body of knowledge backed up by religion. Moral teaching, therefore, if it is to be a genuine enlightenment of practical reason, must not leave religion out of account; it must be given with a religious inspiration. This does not mean that moral rules should be presented only as dictated by religion. On the contrary, the reasons which make them necessary for human life should be ceaselessly stressed, as well as their natural foundations and suitabilities. Morality is steeped in intelligence, the goal is to awaken moral intelligence in the pupil. I think that the discussion of concrete instances, taken from ordinary life, and of particular *points of conscience* is better calculated to sharpen ethical awareness as well as to interest the child than mere emphasis on general principles. Discussions of this kind, relying upon the natural moral instinct of the youth, and asking his active participation, seem to me especially adapted for the first years of training in moral knowledge. Later on deeper and more general considerations would be embarked upon. Conformably to the chief importance of the matter, such moral teaching, both rationally developed and religiously inspired, should form the subject of special courses in the curriculum of schools and colleges.

It has moreover to remain distinct—I mean after the years of early formation—from religious training itself, which implies many other subject-matters than morality and must be more concerned with God than with man. I may run counter to the conventions of contemporary education, yet it is my own conviction that this religious training should not only be given in the family and the church-community, but should also be an integral part of the life of the school. I do not see how we can pretend that God has less right to have his place in the school than Euclid or Professor John Dewey. And it is the right of the child to be allowed to acquire through his formal education religious knowledge as well as any knowledge which plays an essential part in the life of man.

Such are the principles which dominate the question. They are, to my mind, grounded in the nature of things. If they are still disregarded by many, this is, in my opinion, mainly as a result of the difficulties involved in their application, and because of the interference of other principles, such as the lay or merely temporal character of the state.

Yet I am convinced that these difficulties may be overcome without the latter principle being denied or imperiled. With the denominational schools, colleges or universities, the problem of religious training and of moral teaching given in connection with religion is obviously solved from the very start. Even the whole structure of education should be inspired by the very philosophy of life and the fundamental outlook proper to the denomination of the school, which is a prominent advantage from the religious and spiritual point of view. The problem is rather to avoid youth's being ignorant or even distrustful of those who are educated in other lines and who will be their fellow-citizens, and to assure among all that mutual understanding which is required by civic friendship and co-operation in the temporal common good. This problem can be easily solved by establishing regular contacts between students of the diverse schools and colleges: either in youth-camps and youth-organizations, or during some periods of common work (for instance, educational visits or travels, common exercise in physical training, etc.), or, as concerns especially universities, by conferences or congresses of students.

Now, if it is a question of nondenominational schools, colleges, and universities, either privately endowed or founded by the city or the state, this time the problem of mutual acquaintance and understanding among youth belonging to different spiritual families is solved from the start. It is the problem of religious and religiously inspired moral teaching which makes difficulties. The general solution consists in having religious training and moral teaching given by diverse teachers, who belong to the different religious creeds in which the students share.

CONCLUSION

What I have discussed in all my previous remarks is what moral teaching should normally be. Now, before concluding, I must add that, as regards moral education, we do not find ourselves in normal conditions. The modern world has met with a complete failure in moral education. As a result, the task of moral re-education is a matter of public emergency. Every serious observer recognizes the fact that children have not only to be trained in behavior, in manner, proper conduct, law observance and politeness, but that this very training remains deficient and precarious if genuine inner formation is not given. In order for teachers in public schools not to face discipline and violence, the theory that children must begin by letting loose and exhausting the instincts of the primitive man does a rather feeble good turn; frank recognition of the authority of teachers, and strong moral principles, that is, taught in utter trust in their truth, surely do more for school discipline than the eventual intervention of police force. I think therefore that, owing to circumstances, additional emphasis should be brought to the teaching of natural morality. The normal way of giving this teaching, which is, as I have pointed out, to have it embodied in the humanities, literature, and history, does not suffice in the face of the tremendous degradation of ethical reason which is today observable. For the moment the evil is still more in intelligence than in behavior, I mean in still civilized countries. Exhausted and bewildered by dint of false and dehumanized philosophy, reason confesses thorough impotence with regard to the justification of any ethical standard. The question is to recover natural and rational adherence of the mind to the most elementary values of human life, to justice, to pity, to freedom. To such a disease of human intelligence and conscience, special remedies should be given, not only by the badly needed revival of religious faith, but also by a revival of the moral power of reason. Accordingly, if teachers may be found whose reason is less sick than that of their students, special teaching should be provided, in schools and colleges, for the principles of natural morality.

At this point I should like to suggest that, according to the nature of things, the field in which natural morality feels most at home, and least deficient, is the field of our temporal activities, or of political, civic, and social morality: because the virtues at play in this field are essentially natural virtues, directed toward the good of civil life or of human civilization, even when they are strengthened by more divine ones; whereas, in the field of personal morality, natural virtues, and the whole trend of moral life, and the very impulse toward the ends of this life cannot be embraced by reason with regard to our real system of conduct in actual existence, unless divine love, which is charity, and the supratemporal destiny of the human person, and the Gospel's virtues, which are grace-given virtues, be also taken into account, and in the first place. As a result, the teaching of natural morality will be inclined, in virtue of its own object, to lay stress on what may be called the ethics of political life and of civilization. Which is all to the good (for here it enjoys its maximum strength and practical truth), on the condition that the teaching of natural morality resist the temptation of neglecting enlightenment about the very root of morality, which is personal morality, and above all the temptation of warping and perverting all its work by making itself a tool of the state and a mere shaping of youth according to the collective pattern supposedly needed by the price, greed or myths of the earthly community.

Chapter Six

SOME TYPICAL ASPECTS
OF CHRISTIAN EDUCATION

THE CHRISTIAN IDEA OF MAN
AND ITS INFLUENCE ON EDUCATION

If we wish to perceive what a Christian philosophy of education consists of, it is clear that the first thing to do is to try to bring out what the Christian idea of man is.

The Christian idea of man has many connotations and implications. Let us point out some of them.

For Christianity there is no transmigration; the immortality of the soul means that after the death of its body the human soul lives forever, keeping its own individuality. It is not enough, moreover, to say that the human soul is immortal; faith holds also that the body will rise up and be united with the soul again; and Thomas Aquinas goes so far as to insist that in the state of separation from its body the soul is no doubt a substance, but one in which human nature does not come to completion; therefore the separate soul does not constitute a person. All this means that soul and body compose one single substantial unit; as against Hinduism and Platonism, Christianity forcefully emphasizes the unity of the human being, and any recurrence of Platonism—for instance the way in which Descartes ("I or my mind") separated the soul (that is, according to him,

Thought or the Mind) from the body (that is, according to him, geometrical Extension) and lodged the mind in the pineal gland, like a waterworks engineer in the midst of his machines—is but a distortion of the Christian idea of man.

Similarly any education of the Cartesian or angelistic type, any education dealing with the child as with a pure mind or a disembodied intellect, despising or ignoring sense and sensation, punishing imagination as a mere power of deception, and disregarding both the unconscious of the instinct and the unconscious of the spirit, is a distortion of the Christian idea of education. Christian education does not worship the human body, as the ancient Greeks did, but it is fully aware of the importance of physical training as aiming at a sound balance of the whole human being; Christian education is intent on making sense-perception, which is the very basis of man's intellectual life, more and more alert, accurate, and integrated; it appeals confidently to the deep, living power of imagination and feeling as well as to the spiritual power of reason; it realizes that in the development of the child hand and mind must be at work together; it stresses the properly human dignity of manual activity.

At this point I am not thinking only of the educational value that the various sorts of crafts taught on the campus have even for future doctors, lawyers, or businessmen. What I mean to say is that, in a more fundamental way, Christian education knows that despite the basic unity of the educational process the task of the school in preparing the young person for adult life is twofold. On the one hand it must provide the equipment in knowledge required by that kind of work—both of the hand and the mind—which the ancients called servile because it is more obviously manual, and which in reality is not servile at all but rather the common human work, the kind of work most natural to man. On the other hand, the school must provide the equipment in knowledge required by that kind of activity—both of the hand and of the mind—which the ancients called liberal because it is more obviously mental, and which should rather be characterized as *more exacting human work*. I shall come back to this question at the end of my lecture, my point being that in our age genuine liberal education should cover both of the two fields I mentioned.

Thus does Christianity lay stress on the fact that man is flesh as well as spirit. But the Christian idea of man has further, and deeper, connotations. Christian faith knows that human nature is good in itself but that it has been put out of order by original sin; hence it is that Christian education will recognize the necessity of a stern discipline, and even of a certain fear, on the condition that this discipline, instead of being merely external—and futile—should appeal to the understanding and the will of the child and become self-discipline, and that this fear should be respect and reverence, not blind animal dread. And Christian faith knows that supernatural grace matters more than original sin and the weakness of human nature, for grace heals and super-elevates nature and makes man participate in divine life itself; hence it is that Christian education will never lose sight of the grace-given equipment of virtues and gifts through which eternal life begins here below. Aware as it is of the fact that in the educational process the vital principle which exists in the student is the "principal agent," while the causality exercised by the teacher is, like medicine, only co-operating and assisting activity, Christian education does not only lay stress on the natural spirituality of which man is capable, it does not only found its entire work on the inner vitality of human nature; it makes its entire work rest also on the vital energies of grace and on the three theological virtues, Faith, Hope, and Charity; and if it is true to its highest aim, it turns man toward grace-given spirituality, toward a participation in the freedom, wisdom, and love of the saints.

A Christian philosophy of man does not see man as a

merely natural being; it sees man as a natural *and* a super-natural being, bearing in itself the pitiful wounds of Adam and the sacred wounds of the Redeemer. There is no natural perfection for man. His perfection is supernatural, the very perfection of that love which is a diffusion of God's love in us, and the example of which Christ gave us in dying for those he loved. The task of the Christian is to enter Christ's work: that is to say, in some way to redeem his fellow-men, spiritually and temporally; and redemption is achieved by the Cross.

Accordingly, Christian education does not tend to make a man naturally perfect, an athletic, self-sufficient hero with all the energies and beauty of nature, impeccable and un-beatable in tennis and football as well as in moral and in-tellectual competitions. It tries to develop as far as possible natural energies and virtues, both intellectual and moral, and tied up with, and quickened by, infused virtues, but it counts more on grace than on nature; it sees man as tending toward the perfection of love despite any possible mistakes and missteps and through the very frailty of nature, praying not to be put to trial and sensing himself a failure, but being at the same time more and more deeply and totally in love with his God and united with Him.

Christian education does not separate divine love from fraternal love, nor does it separate the effort toward self-per-fection and personal salvation of others. And Christian edu-cation understands that at every level of human life, from the moral situation of the monk to that of the poet or the political leader, the Christian must take risks more or less great, and is never sheltered, and at the same time must be prepared to fight to the finish for his soul and life in God, using the weapons of the Cross every day. For it is up to us to make any suffering imposed by nature or by men into a merciful cross, if only we freely and obediently accept it in love. And furthermore the cross is there, at each and every moment in our life when we have to undergo that rending and agony in which, even with respect to small things, the choice between good and evil consists.

All this does not concern adult life only or adult education only; it begins in a more or less dim way very early for man. That is why the integral idea of Christian education, the idea of Christian education in its wholeness and as a lifelong process, already applies to the child in a way adapted to his condition, and must guide school education as to the general orientation of the educational process and the first beginnings of which the child is capable.

THE REQUIREMENTS OF CHRISTIAN EDUCATION

I should like to distinguish in Christian education two categories of requirements. In the first place Christian education involves all those requirements which characterize in general any genuine education truly aiming at helping a child or man attain his full formation or his completeness as a man. I have discussed these general points on other occasions and do not intend to do so today. In the second place Christian education, insofar as it is precisely Christian, has a number of specific requirements, dependent on the fact that the young person with whom it is concerned is a Christian and must be prepared to lead his adult life as a Christian. It is with respect to this second category of requirements that I shall now submit some observations. The first point will have to do with the curriculum in general; the second, with the development of Christian intelligence; the third, with the ways in which religious knowledge and spiritual life are to be fostered.

The first point has to do with the problem of Christian culture raised by Mr. Christopher Dawson in several interesting and challenging articles.[1] Is a curriculum in the

[1] Cf. Christopher Dawson, "Education and Christian Culture," *The Commonweal*, (Dec. 4, 1953); "Problems of Christian Culture," *The Common-*

humanities fitted to the education of a Christian if it is only
or mainly occupied with the Graeco-Roman tradition and
pagan or merely secular authors?

Before tackling the question I cannot help remembering
that the teacher in philosophy of the Angelic Doctor was the
pagan Aristotle. In a more general way, and in relation to
deeper considerations, I should like to observe that in general one of the aspects of the universality proper to Christianity is the fact that Christianity encompasses the whole
of human life in all its states and conditions; Christianity is
not a sect, not even in the sense of a sect dedicated to the
purest perfection. Let us think for instance of those Essenes
who a few centuries before Christ lived up to high moral
standards and about whom we have learned many interesting details from recent archaeological discoveries. The Essenes were a closed group, a sect. Christians are not a sect,
and this is the very paradox of Christianity; Christianity says,
Be perfect as your heavenly Father is perfect, and Christianity gives this precept not to a closed group but to all men,
whatever their state of life may be, even to those among us
who are most deeply engaged in the affairs and seductions
of this world. That is why, required as they are to tend to
the perfection of love, Christians, as I observed a moment
ago, have to confront the world and to take risks at every
stage or degree of human existence and human culture. They
are not of the world but they are in the world, as really and
profoundly *in* as any man can be. They must be secluded
from nothing, save from evil. All the riches of Egypt are
theirs. Everything valuable for man and for the human mind
belongs to them, who belong to Christ.

Coming now to education and our problem of Christian
culture in the curriculum, I would say that in my opinion
what is demanded is to get rid of those absurd prejudices
which can be traced back to the Renaissance and which

weal (April 15, 1955). (*Editors' Note:* See also Dawson's book, *The Crisis of Western Education.* New York: Sheed and Ward, 1961.)

banish from the blessed land of educational curricula a number of authors and matters under the pretext that they are specifically religious, and therefore not "classical," though they matter essentially to the common treasure of culture. The writings of the Fathers of the Church are an integral part of the humanities as well as, or more than, those of the Elizabethan dramatists; St. Augustine and Pascal matter to us no less than Lucretius or Marcus Aurelius. It is important for young people to know the history of astronomy or the history of Greek and Latin literature, but it is at least as important for them to know the history of the great theological controversies and the history of those works about spiritual life and mystical experience which have been for centuries jewels of Christian literature.

Yet, it is my conviction as well as Christopher Dawson's that, once this point has been clearly established, the curriculum in the humanities of a Christian college must deal still more than that of a secular college with the whole of human culture. The significant thing, and what causes our approach to be Christian, is the perspective and inspiration, the *light* in which all this is viewed.[2] To know the great works produced by the human mind in any spiritual climate —and not only as a matter of information but in order to understand their significance and to *situate* them in the great starry universe of the intellect—is a requirement of that very universality of Christianity which I just spoke of. To tell the truth, that with which the traditional, classical Graeco-Roman humanities are to be reproached is mainly their narrowness and *provincialism*. In our age the humanities do not only extend beyond literature; they extend beyond the West-

---

[2] ". . . the sociological problem of a Christian culture is also the psychological problem of integration and spiritual health. I am convinced that this is the key issue. Personally I would prefer a Ghetto culture to no religious culture at all, but under modern conditions the Ghetto solution is no longer really practicable. We must make an effort to achieve an open Catholic culture which is sufficiently conscious of the value of its own tradition to be able to meet secularist culture on an equal footing." Dawson, "Problems of Christian Culture," p. 36.

ern world and Western culture, they must be concerned
with the achievements of the human mind in every great
area of civilization; nay, more, with the prime and basic
human apperceptions and discoveries which are obscurely
contained in the myths and symbolic imagination of primitive men. Our watchword should be enlargement, Christian-
inspired enlargement, not narrowing, even Christian-centered narrowing, of the humanities. The history of civilizations, and anthropology, may play in this connection—here
again I am in agreement with Christopher Dawson—a basic
introductory part, if they are viewed and understood in an
authentic philosophical and theological light.

Incidentally, I should like to touch upon another question, which does not have to do with the humanities but
rather with that notion of Christian inspiration and Christian light which I just alluded to. It is obvious that any matter dealing with the meaning of existence or the destiny of
man can be illumined by Christian inspiration. But what
about all these matters in which no metaphysical or moral
value is involved? Has the notion of Christian inspiration or
the idea of Christian education the slightest significance
when it comes to the teaching of mathematics, astronomy,
or engineering? The answer, I think, is that there are of
course no Christian mathematics or Christian astronomy or
engineering; but if the teacher has Christian wisdom, and if
his teaching overflows from a soul dedicated to contemplation, the *mode* or manner in which his teaching is given—in
other words, the mode or manner in which his own soul and
mind perform a living and illuminating action on the soul
and mind of another human being—will convey to the student and awaken in him something *beyond* mathematics,
astronomy, or engineering: first, a sense of the proper place
of these disciplines in the universe of knowledge and human
thought; second, an unspoken intimation of the immortal
value of truth, and of those rational laws and harmony which

are at play in things and whose primary roots are in the divine intellect.

The second point relating to the requirements of Christian education as such is concerned with the development of Christian intelligence. May I recall a saying of a great Dominican friar, Father Clérissac, who was my first guide and to whom I shall always feel indebted? *"La vie chrétienne est à base d'intelligence,"* he said. "Intelligence is the very basis of Christian life." If it is true that school training has primarily to do with the intellect and the equipment of intelligence, this saying of Father Clérissac is for Christian educators a clear warning of the particular importance of school training, assuming that school training does not prove false to its ideal essence.

In this connection, what is true of education in general is especially true of Christian education. It is a sacred obligation for a Christian school or college to keep alive the sense of truth in the student; to respect his intellectual and spiritual aspirations and every beginning in him of creative activity and personal grasping of reality; never, as St. Thomas puts it, to dig a pit before him without filling it up, to appeal to the intuitive power of his mind, and to offer to him a unified and integrated universe of knowledge.

It is not irrelevant to expose at this point an illusion which seems to me to be particularly insidious. Just as it is often believed that in society no human person, no man invested with public office and charged with applying the law, but only the law itself, that abstract entity which is the law, has to be obeyed and to exert authority, so it is often believed that in the school no human person, no man invested with teaching authority and charged with conveying science, but only science or scholarship itself, that abstract entity which is science or scholarship, has to be listened to and to exercise the task of instructing minds. As a result, many teachers hold that it is their duty to dissemble and put aside as far as possible, or even to atrophy, their own convictions, which are the convictions of a given man, not the pronouncements of abstract science or scholarship. And since these so-called pronouncements exist only in the books written by the various scholars, and in the form (as a rule, and especially when it comes to the humanities and philosophy) of conflicting statements, the task of the teacher, modestly throwing himself into the shade, boils down to presenting to the student a carefully and objectively prepared picture of incompatible opinions, between which only subjective taste or feeling appears apt to choose. What is the effect of such teaching? To blunt or kill all that I have just described as requiring a sacred attention from the teacher, and to make the student grope from pit to pit. The first duty of a teacher is to develop within himself, for the sake of truth, deep-rooted convictions, and frankly to manifest them, while taking pleasure, of course, in having the student develop, possibly against them, his own personal convictions.

Let me now turn our attention toward a distinction which has, to my mind, crucial practical importance; namely, the distinction which I have emphasized elsewhere between natural intelligence, or intelligence with its native power only, and intelligence perfected by intellectual virtues, that is by those acquired qualities or energies which are peculiar to the scientist, the artist, the philosopher, etc. My contention is that intellectual virtues and skills, which are terribly exacting and require therefore an absorbing special training, are to be acquired during the period of graduate or advanced study, whereas school and college education is the proper domain of natural intelligence, which thirsts for universal knowledge and progresses more spontaneously than technically or scientifically, in vital unity with imagination and poetic sensibility. Hence the notion of *basic liberal education,* which is concerned with *universal knowledge* because it has essentially to do with *natural intelligence,* and which does not try to make the child into a scholar, a physicist, a composer, etc., albeit in a diminutive way, but endeavors only to make him understand the *meaning* and grasp the basic truth of the various disciplines in which universal knowledge is interested. As a result, the scope of the liberal arts and the humanities would be greatly enlarged, so as to comprise, according to the requirements of modern intelligence, physics and the natural sciences, the history of sciences, anthropology and the other human sciences, with the history of cultures and civilizations, even technology (insofar as the activity of the spirit is involved) and the history of manual work and the arts, both mechanical and fine arts. But on the other hand, and to compensate for this enlargement, the manner of teaching and the quantitative, material weight of the curriculum, as regards each of the disciplines in question, would be made less heavy: for any effort to cram the mind of the student with facts and figures, and with the so-called integrity of the subject matter, by dint of useless memorization or shallow and piecemeal information, would be definitely given up; and the great thing would be to develop in the young person genuine understanding of, and active participation in, the truth of the matter, and those primordial intuitions through which what is essentially illuminating as to the basic verities of each discipline learned is definitely and unshakably possessed.

As applied to Christian education, the aforementioned remarks have, it seems to me, a special bearing on the teaching of philosophy and theology, both of which should be the keystone of the edifice of learning in a Christian college, dedicated as it is, by definition, to wisdom. Common sense and natural intelligence, sharpened by the infused virtue of faith, are enough—not to be a philosopher and a theologian, to be sure, but to understand philosophy and theology, intelligently taught. Philosophical training, as I see it, might be composed of two main courses, supporting one another: on the one hand, a course in the relatively few basic philosophical problems, as viewed and illumined in the perspective of Christian philosophy and as related to the most pressing questions with which the age is concerned; on the other hand, a course in the history of philosophy, intent on bringing out the central intuition in which every great system originates and the more often than not wrong conceptualization which makes these systems irreducibly antagonistic.

As to theology, it is not to form a future priest or minister that it has to be taught in a Christian college, it is to equip the layman's reason in such a way that he will grasp the content of his own faith in a deeper and more articulate manner, and use the light and wisdom of a supremely unified discipline to solve the problems with which a Christian is confronted in the accomplishment of his mission in temporal society. This theological training, as I see it, should be especially connected with the problems raised by contemporary science, by the great social movements and conflicts of our age, and by anthropology, comparative religion, and the philosophy of culture. I should like to have special seminars in which students in philosophy and theology would meet representatives of the most various schools of thought: scientists, artists, missionaries, labor leaders, managers, etc. For it is not with books, it is with men that students must be made able to discuss and take their own stand. An inviolable rule would be that, after such meetings, the discussion should continue in further seminars between the students and the teachers of the college, until they have completely mastered the problem and brought out the truth of the matter.

I should like to make a final remark in relation to our present question, namely, the question of the development of Christian intelligence. This remark deals with the Holy Scripture, especially the Old Testament, and modern exegesis. During college years Christian youth should be given serious knowledge of the meaning of exegesis, and of the distinction to be made between what is valid result and discovery and what is arbitrary construction in the exegetical comments of our contemporary scholars. They should be shown how the main problems of exegesis can be solved in the light of a sound theory of divine inspiration, and how our approach to the Biblical text is thus made at the same time more realistic and purer. The question here is not to cultivate vain learning but to go in—with greater awareness of all that is human in the human instrument and greater faith in the divine truth taught by the principal author—for that assiduous reading of the Scriptures which has been a sacred custom in Protestant countries and is now being practiced more and more among Catholics, and which is an invaluable asset of Christian life.

I believe, moreover, that the contact with the Holy Scripture must be at the same time so full of reverence and so deeply personal that it is not advisable to make the teaching of which I am speaking part of the compulsory matters of the curriculum. It would be much better to have this teaching given, as an elective matter, to students really eager to get it, who would constitute for this purpose one of those self-organized groups whose importance I shall stress in a few moments.

There is a third and final point to be made in the second part of this lecture: it has to do with the ways in which religious knowledge and spiritual life are to be fostered in a Christian school or college.

It has often been remarked that, in eighteenth- and nineteenth-century France, for instance, a number of the most violent adversaries of religion had been in their youth either seminarians or pupils of great Jesuit colleges. This is no serious argument against the methods of the seminaries and of the Jesuit Fathers, for, as an old saying puts it, *quid quid recipitur, ad modum recipientis recipitur*—anything that is received is received according to the mood and capacity of the receiver. Yet a more general and surprising fact remains, namely, the fact of the religious ignorance in our contem-

porary world of a great number, I would say of a majority
of people educated in religious schools and denominational
colleges. Why is this so? Because, in my opinion, religious
teaching, however carefully given, remains too much of a
separate, isolated compartment, and is sufficiently integrated
neither with the intellectual interests nor with the personal
life of the students. As a result, it is received by many in
the most superficial stratum of the soul and forgotten almost
as soon as it has been shallowly memorized.

It is through its vital connections with philosophy and
theology that religious training can be really integrated with
the general mental activity and the intellectual interests of
the student. Though a Christian college in which the cosmos
of knowledge is not crowned by theology may have the best
courses in religion, the religious teaching it metes out is but a
leaf which goes with the wind. But it is especially about the
integration of religious training in the personal life of the
students that I should like to say a few words now.

My contention is that the proper way in which such an
integration may be achieved is the development of liturgical
life on the campus and the participation of the student population in the liturgy of the Church.[3] The succession of feasts
which celebrate divine mysteries and the events of our redemption, or commemorate the days on which the saints
have been born to eternity, the prayers, the songs, the sacred
rites of liturgy, compose a kind of immense and uninter-
rupted sign through which the heaven of religious truths
symbolically penetrates our daily life. Breathing in this kind
of heaven provides the student with the oxygen he needs to
have the religious teaching given in the classroom integrated
with the depths of his own personal life.

[3] Cf. *ibid.*, p. 35: ". . . it seems to be clear that the key of the problem
is to be found not in philosophy but in *worship*. . . . In that case the
fundamental 'classics' are not St. Thomas and St. Augustine, but the Bible,
the Missal, the Breviary and the *Acta Sanctorum*." Let us replace "not, but"
by "not only, but also," and all this is true.

I do not wish to see all the students of a Christian college dressed like monks, officiating in the chapel. Nor do I wish to hear all of them, on Sundays, collectively answer the priest at Mass—I am afraid the automatic display of the vociferations of boys or the cooing of girls is more liable to disturb than to quicken adoration and thanksgiving. What I wish is to have liturgical-study groups freely organized on the campus, and to have a certain number of the members of these groups, inspired by the example of the Benedictine monks, form sorts of brotherhoods and choirs in order actively to participate in liturgical ceremonies, especially in the celebration of High Mass. Thus, I assume, a sufficient emulation or stimulation regarding liturgical life would take place in the whole student population.

The best things must develop on a free basis. It is so with liturgical life, it is so with daily attendance at Mass and the reception of Holy Communion. (I note in passing the striking improvement which it has been possible to observe in the student population of Notre Dame University, after it was decided to give the Eucharist in all the chapels of the campus and at any time in the morning to any student desiring to receive it.) In the groups of which I am now speaking, whose aim would be the knowledge and practice of liturgy, a brief seminar would be held every day on the lives of the saints mentioned in the Breviary.

Next to these liturgical groups there would be other groups, probably fewer in number but exercising a more important action as a hidden ferment, which would be dedicated to studying the doctrine of theologians and great spiritual writers on mental prayer and mystical experience, and learning the rudiments of contemplative wisdom. I think that the most useful task of such groups would be to foster among their members that daily reading of the Gospel which is the normal way toward wordless prayer and the very nourishment of spiritual life.

TWO IMPORTANT ISSUES

In this third and last part of my lecture, I should like to discuss two issues: first, concerning the moral formation of the youth; secondly, concerning liberal education for all.

With respect to the first issue, it is to be noticed that school or college education is only a part and a beginning of man's education, especially because it is more concerned with intelligence and knowledge than with the will and moral virtues, or with telling young people how to think than with telling them how to live. According to the nature of things, moral education is more the task of the family, assisted by the religious community to which it belongs, than the task of the school.

Now what is normal in itself is not always what occurs most often in fact. As a matter of fact, it is too easy to observe today that, especially in the social and moral conditions created by our industrial civilization, the family group happens frequently to fail in its moral duty toward children, and appears more liable either to wound them or at least to forsake them in their moral life than to educate them in this domain. Thus the school has, in some imperfect and partial way, to try to make up for the lacks of the family group in the moral formation of youth. But what can be the power and efficacy of teaching and classrooms in such matters?

It is at this point that we may realize the crucial importance of the grouping of students in self-organized teams. In my essay, "Thomist Views on Education," I have already insisted on the part to be played by these teams in the life of that kind of republic which the school or the college is.[4] The teams in question are different in purpose and in structure from the study groups whose role is also essential in academic life and some examples of which we have just con-

4 See p. 68.

sidered. These self-organized teams, of which I am now speaking, are responsible for the discipline of the students and their academic progress. Through their captains, whom they themselves elect, they convey to the school authorities their experiences and problems, and their suggestions regarding the organization of studies and the general discipline.

But in a Christian college—and this is my point—the self-organized teams which I have just described would also have another and more essential function. They would have to enforce and carry into being, in all occasions and incidents of daily existence, the requirements of Christian charity. It is on the exercise of mutual charity that the attention of everyone in them would be focused. And so these teams would make up in some way for what might be lacking in the moral education provided by the family—and they would be, so to speak, workshops in the evangelical rules of mutual love.

To make things more precise, let me point out a custom which the teams in question might find the greatest advantage in borrowing from the daily life of religious orders. The custom I have in mind is that of the *chapter*, in which all the members of a religious community gather together for the purpose of a common self-examination. Each one must make known the faults—not, of course, the faults depending on the *forum internum*, the inner tribunal of conscience, but those depending on the *forum externum*—that he has committed during the day; and each one has similarly to make known the same kind of external, visible faults or mistakes he has observed in others. There is thus a sort of general washing, presided over by the abbot or prior, who metes out the soap of suitable exhortation: thereafter everyone goes back smart and lively into his own cell. Well, our self-organized teams, as I see them, would imitate this wise custom, fittingly adopted or modified, and hold chapters of their own—I know of Christian families which did so for many years, and with considerable moral profit—laying stress especially on all that

concerns the requirements of mutual respect and love in the
matters of conscience, be they serious or minor, of which the
group is made aware. And the captain of the team would
play the part of the prior in giving the moral direction and
explanations he deems necessary. The benefit of the custom
is twofold: I mean to say, on the one hand the development
of the sense of responsibility and moral awareness, and the
progress in Christian charity; and on the other hand the
psychological relief caused by the fact of giving expression
to that perception and experience of the lacks of others
which, if they had to remain repressed, might, slight as the
matter may be, embitter one's soul.

All this talk about self-organized teams is not simply theoretical. I have personally known a place in which the experiment was made, and with full success.

I have emphasized the importance of two different kinds
of self-organized groups: the self-organized teams of students
of which I just spoke, concerned with the moral and political
life of the educational republic, and operating independently from teachers; and the self-organized study groups,
which could and should develop in connection with a large
variety of matters, and in which the teachers play a necessary part, but more as counselors and guides than as professors and lecturers. When I think of the necessity of these
diverse self-organized groups and of the way in which they
are likely to grow in actual fact, in proportion as their
significance is recognized, I come to the idea that the educational structure of future schools and colleges will be different from the present one: instead of one single system, there
would be two co-ordinated systems of forces or formative
energy—two nervous systems, so to speak, confronting and
complementing one another; the first system being composed
of those various centers, starting from above, of teaching
authority which are the faculties, departments, schools or institutes; the second being composed of those various centers,
starting from below, of autonomous study and self-discipline

which are our freely self-organized groups or teams of students. The unity which schools and universities are looking for[5] is not a unity of mechanical centralization; it is a spontaneous, star-studded unity of harmony in diversity.

By way of conclusion I have still a few remarks to submit about the other issue I have mentioned, namely the question of liberal education for all.

The notion of liberal education for all is, in my opinion, one of those concepts which are in themselves close to the requirements of natural law, and appear obviously valid once we think them over, but which were long repressed, so to speak, or prevented from being uttered in consciousness, because social conditions and social prejudice, condemning the greater number of men to a kind of enslaved life, made such concepts impracticable, which is as much as to say unthinkable. This concept of liberal education for all is a late fructification of a Christian principle; it is intimately related to the Christian idea of the spiritual dignity of man and the basic equality of all men before God. Education directed toward wisdom, and centered on the humanities, is education for freedom. Every human being, whatever his particular vocation may be, is entitled to receive such a properly human and humanistic education. No educational philosophy should be more dedicated to the ideal of liberal education for all than the Christian philosophy of education.

Coming now to practical application, I must first of all make clear that in saying "liberal education for all," it is of *basic* liberal education—basic liberal education for all—that I am thinking. This concept of basic liberal education has already been stressed above. It gives practical value and feasibility to the concept of liberal education for all. For on the one hand basic liberal education, covering as it does the field of the achievements of the human mind in science as well as in literature and art, has nothing to do with the old notion of liberal education as an almost exclusively lit-

5 Cf. John U. Nef, *The Universities Look for Unity*, New York, 1943.

erary education. On the other hand the resulting broadening of the matters of the curriculum is compensated for by a considerable alleviation in the very approach to these matters, which is henceforth adjusted to the needs and capacity of natural intelligence—more intuitive, therefore, and freed from any burden of pseudo-science. As far as the college years are concerned, it would be normal, as we have already pointed out,[6] to have the college divided into a number of fields of concentration or of primary interest, each represented by a school. The college would thus be divided into a number of *schools of oriented humanities* all devoted to liberal education but oriented to the particular intellectual virtue or skill which the students had chosen to develop.

But what about the main difficulty, namely the fact that for many boys and girls intellectual life, liberal arts, and the humanities are only a bore, and that as a result liberal education, in proportion as it is extended to a greater and greater number of young people, seems condemned to degenerate and fall to lower and lower levels? I am far from believing that all the boys and girls in question should be rated as duller students. In any case it may be answered that good educational methods are intended to stimulate the natural interests and intelligence of normal students, not to make the dull ones meet the standards. The clear maxim in these matters is, as Mortimer Adler put it in his seminar on education, "The best education for the most gifted person in the community is, in its equivalent form, the best education for all."[7] As a rule, to ask men to maintain themselves at a level of real humanity is to ask a little too much of them, a little more than they are capable of. That is why what have been called heterogeneous schools or classes (segregating the brighter and the duller) must be considered a bad solution in every respect. Better to have homogeneous courses—I

[6] See p. 73.

[7] "Seminar on Education in a Modern Industrial Democracy," Philadelphia, June 19 and 20, 1952 (unpublished).

mean adapted, according to the principle I have just mentioned, to the highest possible level with respect to the capacity not of the duller, but of the good average student; and to assist in a special way the brighter students by allowing them freely to group together in extracurricular units —study clubs or academies—under some tutorial guidance.

All that is true, but it is insufficient and does not reach the root of the matter. It is necessary to go further. As long as the problem is posed in the usual terms of classical education, I mean in terms of the student's greater or lesser capacity to enjoy the pure activities of the intellect and progress in them—in other words, as long as pure intellectual activity is considered the only activity worthy of man, and those who do not enjoy it are considered to be necessarily duller—no really satisfactory answer can be given. A deeper and more general principle must be brought to the fore. What principle? The Christian principle of the dignity of manual activity. This principle, which the monks of former times perfectly understood, was long disregarded by reason of social structure and ideological prejudice, both of which kept more or less the imprint of the times when manual labor was the job of slaves (as is still manifest in the expression "servile work"). As against such prejudice, let us not forget that St. Paul made a living as a tent-maker—not to speak of Jesus Himself, Who was a carpenter. The principle of the dignity and human value of manual work is now in the process of being at last realized by common consciousness. We have to understand that genuine manual work is neither the work of a beast of burden nor that of a robot, but human work in which both body and mind are at play—as they are also in the intellectual work of a writer, a lawyer, a teacher, a doctor, etc., who cannot perform his own task without a certain dose of bodily exertion. The difference is that in one case (manual work) bodily activity plays the part of a (secondary) "principal agent" activated by the mind, and in the other case (intellectual work) the part of a merely "instrumental agent" moved by the mind. So both are, like man, made of flesh and spirit; manual work and intellectual work are equally human in the truest sense and directed toward helping man to achieve freedom. We have good reasons to believe that a general rehabilitation of manual work will characterize the next period of our industrial civilization.

If we take all these things into consideration, we shall see that such a crucial change in perspective, which is Christian in itself and in its first origin, will inevitably reverberate in education, and must be of special interest for the Christian philosophy of education; and we shall realize better the bearing of the remarks that I submitted at the beginning of this lecture, when I observed that the task of the school in preparing the young person for adult life must involve a twofold function: on the one hand it must provide the equipment in knowledge required by the vocations and activities which consist mainly of manual work; on the other hand it must provide the equipment in knowledge required by those vocations and activities which consist mainly of intellectual work.

These things have been recognized for centuries, but the result has been an invidious opposition between a so-called *popular* education, preparing for manual vocations, and *liberal* education. My point is that in a somewhat distant future *liberal* education, on the contrary, will permeate the whole of education, whether young people are prepared for manual or for intellectual vocations. In other words popular education must become liberal, and liberal education must become popular. Is it not clear that "liberal education for all" means liberal education for prospective manual workers as well as for prospective intellectual workers? The very possibility of this supposes considerable changes in our social and educational structures, a result of which would be to make some more democratic, probably gratis equivalent of our present colleges available to all.

The *unipolar* conception of liberal education would then

be replaced by a *bipolar* conception; and here we have the answer to our problem. We would no longer have to choose between either obliging students unconcerned with disinterested knowledge to trudge along in the rear of classes which are a bore to them or diverting them toward other and supposedly inferior studies by reason of a lack, or a lesser capacity. We would have these students enter into a different but equally esteemed and appreciated system of study, and steer spontaneously, by reason of a positive preference, enjoyment, and capacity, for a type of liberal education which, while remaining essentially concerned with humanities, prepares them for some vocation pertaining to manual work—not, of course, by making them apprentices in any of the innumerable manual vocations but rather by teaching them, theoretically and practically, matters concerning the general categories into which manual service can be divided, such as farming, mining, craftsmanship, the various types of modern industrial labor, etc.

Thus education, especially college education, would be organized around two opposite centers, a center of manual-service training, and a center of intellectual-service training, each one with its own various institutes or schools of oriented humanities. And though intellectual service is in itself or in its nature more spiritual and therefore of greater worth than manual service, the fact remains that with respect to man and therefore to the humanities the one and the other are equally worthy of our esteem and devotion and equally apt to help us fulfill our destiny. They would be on a completely equal footing in the educational system.

As I see it, the choice between the two master directions I have just pointed out would take place preferably at the end of high school, possibly earlier or later. And the two centers in question could materialize either in one single, sufficiently large institution or in a variety of different colleges, vocational institutes, or advanced schools specializing in one matter or another. The important thing, moreover, is that in any case manual-service training as well as intellectual-service training should be permeated with liberal arts and the humanities, though in a different way.

Of course some dull or lazy or psychologically inept people would always be found in one place as well as in the other. But I am convinced that interest, intellectual curiosity, and understanding with respect to the whole field of the humanities and liberal arts would exist as a rule in the students of the manual-service training as well as in those of the other center, on the condition that the mode or way of approach be fittingly adapted. For if to most of these students matters pertaining to disinterested knowledge, the liberal arts, and humanities are liable to appear a bore, it is only insofar as they are matters of *formal teaching*. If the approach becomes informal and unsystematic, everything changes for them.

In my book, *Education at the Crossroads*, I laid stress on the division between the *activities of learning* and the *activities of play* in the school, and on the essential part which play has in school life.[8] For play possesses a value and worth of its own, being activity of free expansion and a gleam of poetry in the very field of those energies which tend by nature toward utility.

Now I would like to go much farther than I did in that book, and, while broadening considerably the notion of the activity of play so as to comprise in it the notion of *informal* and *unsystematic* learning, I would submit that, on the one hand, training in matters which are of most worth and have primacy in importance may take place through the instrumentality of the activities of play as well as of the activities of learning; and, on the other hand, the relationship between activities of learning and activities of play would be reversed or opposite in the schools of the intellectual-service training center and in those of the manual-service training center. In the first case the humanities, liberal arts, and philosophy

[8] *Education at the Crossroads*, p. 55.

are matters of formal learning; and craftsmanship, for instance, and any kind of manual work, including painting and sculpture, are matters of informal learning or play. In the second case it is the manifold field of manual-service training which would be a matter of formal and systematic learning, whereas the humanities, liberal arts, and philosophy would be matters of informal learning or play: a situation which would in no way mean any diminution in intrinsic importance but which would quicken and set free the intellectual interest and understanding of the category of students in question with respect to these things.

My working hypothesis, then, is that in the schools of the manual-service training center education in all matters pertaining to the humanities and liberal arts would be surprisingly successful if it were given not by way of formal teaching but by way of play and informal learning. With respect to informal learning, I would say that the teaching (formal teaching) of gardening, for instance, offers every opportunity to give students, by way of digressions or comments, a most fruitful informal and unsystematic teaching in botany and biology, not to speak of economics, the history of architecture, the history of civilization, etc. It is the same with the teaching (formal teaching) of the various skills and kinds of knowledge required from labor by modern industry and the informal and unsystematic teaching of physics and chemistry, nuclear physics, engineering, mathematics.

With respect to play, I would say that facilities given to students to read books of their own choice and for their own pleasure, then seminars in these readings, in literature, in philosophy, then concerts and theatrical performances with appropriate comments, all these things conceived of and managed as a preparation for having the adult worker make profitable use of his leisure time constitute a genuine education in the humanities and intellectual life in the form of that activity of free expansion which characterizes play.

Chapter Seven

THE EDUCATION OF WOMEN

Culture today stands in need of defense. For this defense we need wealth, material resources, industrial, technological and scientific equipment of the most perfect kind. All of these things are means in the service of culture. But culture itself consists in knowing *how* and *why* to use these things for the good of the human being and the securing of his liberty. Culture is essentially the inner forming of man. This forming is achieved by the development within us of what constitutes human strength above all else, of those inner powers which the people of former times called the virtues, virtues of the mind, and virtues of the heart. The power of the soul is an immaterial power which cannot be beaten down by shells and machine-guns. The soul yields only when it so wills. Culture implies the pursuit of human happiness, but it requires also that we know in what this happiness consists. Thus the primary insistence must be on that kind of knowledge we call *disinterested*, for this is the knowledge which has to do with our supreme interests, interests which arise above the present moment. Culture consists in knowing, but it does not consist only in knowing: it consists even more in *having known*, and in the forgetting of a great many things because we know them too well and because they have passed down from memory into the very marrow of our bones. Culture implies the possessing of the means of liberty, but first it implies being inwardly free. "*Science sans conscience n'est que ruine de l'âme*" ("Knowledge without conscience is the destruction of the soul"),[1] Rabelais said long ago. The richest and most beautiful of cultures is nothing if moral development does not keep pace with the scientific and artistic development, if man is not conscious of the reasons he has for living, and the reasons he has for dying; this is the great tradition of your pioneers and the founders of your Republic, and that is why your land is so dear to all who cherish human liberty.

I know that everything is not learned at school and that there are many things that cannot be taught either through books or through lectures. But I do know, too, that books and lectures are an indispensable and basic vehicle of what man should know, and that without schools worthy of the name there is no culture. The primary purpose of schools, colleges, universities, of education in general, is not to teach us how *to do* something, but rather first to furnish us with the means, and especially the knowledge, which enable us to learn how *to be* in accordance with all the formative qualities and lasting perfections of soul and mind. "We must *be* something before *doing* something," said Goethe, and the Scholastic philosophers before him said that action follows being. Education teaches us how to be something, that is to say, to be persons truly human. In those colleges whose program corresponds to that intellectual ensemble which the people of long ago called liberal arts, this task of the schools appears in a way especially manifest. Let me add that the mission of the school respecting culture is as great, in a sense even greater, in women's colleges than in men's.

Men have many things *to do*, they will have to do these things with a vengeance in the age we are now entering, in which so much that is in ruins must be reconstructed.

---

[1] See *Gargantua and Pantagruel,* Bk. II, Ch. 8.

Women have to a slightly greater degree, and will preserve to a slightly greater degree, the leisure of *being*. This is their great privilege, and a great duty. Two things strike the foreign observer who visits America; this country appears to him as the privileged land of youth, and the privileged land of womanhood. Youth is honored here, and youth is served, especially in the colleges, in a more liberal and generous way than in many other countries. Womanhood is honored here, and her liberty and dignity are respected in a more ample and uncompromising way than in many other countries. Women here have a deep sense of their own mission with respect to culture. The teaching of young women appears hence as a thing doubly important and significant in the American way of life.

The recognition of equality of rights for women as well as for men marks a great human conquest and the foremost of these rights is the cultivation of the mind. The very fact that the same instruction and like opportunities of access to the highest fields of knowledge should be given to young ladies and young men, with such excellent results as we see in this country, is in itself the refutation of out-of-date notions about the intellectual possibilities of women. Nevertheless this fundamental equality of the human intellect in man and woman, since it is a living and creative equality, admits of profound differentiations, which, as far as the things of culture are concerned, are decidedly not to the disadvantage of woman. My already long experience as a professor has shown me that often young women enter into the realm of knowledge with an intellectual passion more ardent and a love of truth more disinterested than young men do. If they are usually less gifted than men for constructive syntheses and the inventive work of reason, they possess over them the advantage of a more vital and organic feeling for knowledge. When they love truth, it is in order to bring down truth into life itself. When they love philosophy, it is because it helps them to discover themselves and the meaning of existence; and they well understand the saying of Plato, that we must philosophize with our whole soul. Their mind is less compartmentalized than that of man; they have, when they are not too flighty, a greater need of unity; and this is the reason, too, that an education too departmentalized is even more harmful to them than to young men. M. Bergson thinks that it is an illusion to believe that women are more gentle and compassionate than men, and I suppose he is right. In return they are often less naïve and more courageous in the face of public opinion.

In truth, the complete human being implies the duality of feminine and masculine qualities. In the order of the spirit, these qualities are complementary. In a general way, we can say that man is gifted in the functions of judgment, woman in those of intuition. Without the treasure of perceptions, images, stimulating problems and intuitive proddings which women interpose ceaselessly into the world, and which they endlessly bring before us, sometimes in a way very disconcerting to our tranquility, human culture would become poor indeed. Upon them, above all, depends that mysterious spiritual wealth—unutterable and substantial, sorrowful, too —which we call *experience,* and which plays a role so essential in culture, which renders it lasting and fecund, enabling it, as in fine wines, to grow older while all the while it becomes more delightful. These hasty remarks enable us to understand how the teaching of the same discipline is received in a different way by young women and young men, and how by dispensing to both the same capital of knowledge and wisdom, this teaching is established here and there in a highly characteristic spiritual climate. Happy differences which blend together for the perfecting of culture and the human person!

Perhaps the young women of this time do not sufficiently realize the long endeavors and long sufferings which have been necessary in order to bring the human person, in woman as in man, to a consciousness of its dignity. Christianity has played a great part in this story. The emancipation of woman began when the Gospel was preached to all, Greeks and Jews, poor and rich, male and female, as to beings called to the same divine life and the same liberty of the children of God. The sense of human dignity is the mark of every civilization of Christian origin and foundation, even when our fickleness of mind causes us to forget it. Little by little mankind has understood that, not only with regard to supernatural values, but also in the order of natural values and of earthly civilization, the human person, even though it be part of the political community, has within itself values and a calling which transcend the political community, for they are things which rise above time. Truth, beauty, wisdom are sovereignly useful for the State, they are not at the command of the State. The State must serve them, just as the State must respect in each one the fundamental rights of the person. This is the great struggle of our age. The totalitarian enslavement which menaces the world may tear down a great deal, but build up, never, nor even less can it build lastingly, since it proceeds to the annihilation of these essential truths of our nature. A democratic education is not an education which inculcates democratic slogans in children and regiments them for democracy in the manner that a fascist education inculcates fascist slogans in children and regiments them for the service of the fascist State. To train along lines inspired by animal training is precisely the special mark of the totalitarian states. We do not envy them this privilege. Let them keep it! They will die of it. A democratic education is an education which helps human persons to shape themselves, judge by themselves, discipline themselves, to love and to prize the high truths which are the very root and safeguard of their dignity, to respect in themselves and in others human nature and conscience, and to conquer themselves in order to win their liberty.

Chapter Eight

THE CONQUEST OF FREEDOM

FREEDOM OF INDEPENDENCE AND FREEDOM OF CHOICE

In this essay I shall not treat of free will or freedom of choice. The existence and value of this kind of freedom are, however, taken for granted in all I shall say. That is why I shall first give a few brief indications in their regard. The freedom I shall treat of subsequently is the freedom of independence and of exultation, which can be called also—in a Paulinian but not Kantian sense—freedom of autonomy, or also, freedom of expansion of the human person. It takes for granted the existence of freedom of choice in us, but it is substantially distinct from it.

A badly constructed philosophical theory that falsifies the second operation by which the mind of man knows itself explicitly, can counteract and paralyze the primary and natural operation of spontaneous consciousness. As long as we are not victims of this accident, each of us knows very well *that* he possesses freedom of choice, that is to say, that if we betray a friend, risk our property to aid some unfortunate individual, decide to become a banker, monk, or soldier, these kinds of acts are what they are only because we have involved therein our personality and have arranged that they be so rather than not. But each of us knows very poorly *in what* freedom of choice consists. This obscurity of spontaneous consciousness, unable to bring forth what is implicit in the matter, enables philosophers, and especially savants who philosophize without knowing it, frequently to becloud the question.

Philosophers professing an absolute intellectualism cannot understand the existence of free will because in their eyes intelligence not only precedes will, but precedes it in the manner of a divinity apart, which touches the will without being touched by it and without receiving from it any qualifying action. Hence the domain of formal or specifying determination (what is called the *ordo specificationis*) can never itself depend intrinsically upon the domain of efficiency or existential effectuation (*ordo exercitii*), and the will is reduced to a function by which the intelligence realizes ideas which, in virtue of the mere object they represent, appear best to the subject. Such was the position of the great metaphysicians of the classic age.

Pure empiricists likewise cannot understand the existence of free will, because, recognizing only sensory sequences, the idea of causality exercised by a spirit upon itself has no meaning for them. Hence when they voice an opinion on a question, which, like that of free will, lies essentially in the ontological order, they, as metaphysicians in spite of themselves (and bad ones at that), cannot fail to interpret the empirical results of observational science in the framework of classic mechanism inherited from Spinoza, and give themselves over, without knowing what they are doing, to the most naïve extrapolations. To the extent that science reveals dynamic elements working in our psychical activity, they see in the mere existence of these elements the proof that they operate in a necessarily determining fashion—which is precisely what remains to be proved.

In our times it is Freudianism that offers this empiricist pseudo-metaphysics the greatest possibilities for illusion. I have shown elsewhere[1] that it is very important to distinguish most clearly between the psychoanalytic method, which opens for investigation in the unconscious new roads of the greatest interest, and the philosophy (unconscious of itself) that Freud has sought in crass empiricism, thereby leaving the field of his competence and giving full reign to his dreams. The fact, revealed by psychoanalysis, that there are unconscious motivations which the subject obeys without knowing them furnishes in no manner, as some would imagine, an argument against free will, for free will begins with intellectual judgment and consciousness. To the extent that unconscious motivation makes us act automatically, there is no question of free will; and to the extent that it gives rise to a conscious judgment, the question is whether or not at this moment it fashions this judgment, or by means of free choice is rendered decisively motivating by this judgment. In other words, the question is whether unconscious motivations are necessarily determining or simply contributing, and it is clear that the mere fact of their existence is not sufficient to decide the question.

In general, human free will does not exclude but presupposes the vast and complex dynamism of instincts, tendencies, psycho-physical dispositions, acquired habits, and hereditary traits, and it is at the top point where this dynamism emerges in the world of spirit that freedom of choice is exercised, to give or withhold decisive efficacy to the inclinations and urges of nature. It follows from this that freedom, as well as responsibility, is capable of a multiplicity of degrees of which the Author of being alone is judge. It does not follow from this that freedom does not exist—on the contrary! If it admits of degrees, then it exists.

The efforts of eminent scientists, like Professor Compton, to link indeterminist theories of modern physics to our natu-

[1] Cf. *Quatre Essais sur l'Esprit dans sa Condition Charnelle,* revised edition (Paris: Alsatia, 1956), Chapter I; *Scholasticism and Politics* (New York: Macmillan, 1940), Chapter VI.

ral belief in free will may be highly significant and stimulating to the mind and efficacious in eliminating many prejudices, but I do not think that a strict proof providing this belief with an unshakable intellectual basis can be found in that direction. The direction to follow is metaphysical. It brings us to formulas like those of M. Bergson: "Our motivations are what we make them"; "Our reasons are determined for us only at the moment that they become determining; that is, at the moment when the act is virtually accomplished." But it is not by a philosophy of pure becoming, it is by a philosophy of being and intelligence like that of St. Thomas Aquinas that such formulas receive their full significance and demonstrative value.

Spirit as such implies a sort of infinity; its faculty of desire of itself seeks a good which satisfies absolutely, and therefore to a good without limit, and we cannot have any desire which is not comprehended in this general desire for happiness. But as soon as reflection occurs, our intelligence, confronted with goods that are not the Good, and judging them so, brings into actuality the radical indetermination that our appetite for happiness possesses in regard to everything which is not happiness itself. Efficacious motivation of an intelligent being can be only a practical judgment; and this judgment owes to the will the whole of its efficaciousness; it is will, impelled by its own unpredictable initiative towards the good presented to it by such and such a judgment, that gives this judgment the power of specifying the will efficaciously.

The free act, in which the intelligence and will involve and envelop each other vitally, is thus like an instantaneous flash in which the active and dominating indetermination of the will operates in regard to the judgment itself which determines it; the will can do nothing without an intellectual judgment; and it is will that makes itself determined by judgment and by this judgment rather than by another one.

Far from being a simple function of the intelligence, by which the latter realizes ideas which in virtue of their mere object appear best, the will is an original spiritual energy of infinite capacity which has control over the intelligence and its judgments in the order of practical choice and makes what it wants appear best to the subject *here and now.* What constitutes the real mystery of free will is that while essentially needing intellectual specification, the exercise of the will has primacy over the latter and holds it under its active and dominating indetermination because the will alone can give it existential efficacy.

After this preliminary explanation of freedom of choice, I shall now discuss the freedom of independence.

FREEDOM OF INDEPENDENCE AND THE ASPIRATIONS OF THE PERSON

Human personality is a great metaphysical mystery. We know that an essential characteristic of a civilization worthy of the name is a sense of and respect for the dignity of the human person. We know that to defend the rights and freedom of the human person we must be willing to sacrifice our most precious possessions and our lives. What values, then, deserving of such sacrifice, are enveloped in the personality of man? What do we mean precisely when we speak of the human person? When we say that a man is a person, we do not mean merely that he is an individual, in the sense that an atom, a blade of grass, a fly, or an elephant is an individual. Man is an individual who holds himself in hand by his intelligence and his will; he exists not merely in a physical fashion. He has spiritual superexistence through knowledge and love, so that he is, in a way, a universe in himself, a microcosmos, in which the great universe in its entirety can be encompassed through knowledge. By love he can give himself completely to beings who are to him, as it were, other selves. For this relation no equivalent can be found in the physical world. The human person possesses these characteristics because in the last analysis man, this flesh and these perishable bones which are animated and activated by a divine fire, exists "from the womb to the grave" by virtue of the existence itself of his soul, which dominates time and death. Spirit is the root of personality. The notion of personality thus involves that of totality and independence; no matter how poor and crushed a person may be, he is whole, and as a person, subsistent in an independent manner. To say that a man is a person is to say that in the depths of his being he is more a whole than a part and more independent than servile. It is to say that he is a minute fragment of matter that is at the same time a universe, a beggar who participates in the absolute being, mortal flesh whose value is eternal, and a bit of straw into which heaven enters. It is this metaphysical mystery that religious thought designates when it says that the person is the image of God. The value of the person, his dignity and rights, belong to the order of things naturally sacred which bear the imprint of the Father of Being, and which have in Him the end of their movement.

Freedom of spontaneity, on the other hand, is not, as is free will, a power of choice that transcends all necessity, even interior necessity and all determinism. It does not imply the absence of necessity but merely the absence of constraint. It is the power of acting by virtue of one's own internal inclination and without undergoing the compulsion imposed by an exterior agent.

This kind of freedom admits of all sorts of degrees, from the spontaneity of the electron turning "freely" around a nucleus, that is, without deviating from its path by the interference of a foreign particle, to the spontaneity of the grass in the fields, which grows "freely," and of the bird that flies "freely," that is, obeying only the internal necessities of their nature. When freedom of spontaneity passes the threshold of the spirit and is the spontaneity of a spiritual nature, it becomes properly freedom of independence. To this extent it does not consist merely in following the inclination of nature but in being or making oneself actively the sufficient principle of one's own operation; in other words, in perfecting oneself as an indivisible whole in the act one brings about. This is why freedom of independence exists only in beings which also have free will, and presupposes the exercise of free will in order to arrive at its end.

If the proper sign of personality consists, as I have just said, in the fact of being independent, of being as a whole, it is clear that personality and freedom of independence are related and inseparable. In the scale of being they increase together; at the summit of being God is person in pure act and freedom of independence in pure act. He is so personal that His existence is His very act of knowing and loving, and He is so independent that while causing all things, He Himself is absolutely without cause, His essence being His very act of existence.

In each of us personality and freedom of independence increase together. For man is a being in movement. If he does not augment, he has nothing, and he loses what he had; he must fight for his being. The entire history of his fortunes and misfortunes is the history of his effort to win, together with his own personality, freedom of independence. He is called to the conquest of freedom.

Two basic truths must be noted here. The first is that the human being, though a person and therefore independent because he is a spirit, is, however, by nature at the lowest degree of perfection and independence because he is a spirit united substantially with matter and implacably subject to a bodily condition. Secondly, no matter how miserable, how poor, how enslaved and humiliated he may be, the aspirations of personality in him remain unconquerable; and they tend as such, in the life of each of us as in the life of the human race, toward the conquest of freedom.

The aspirations of personality are of two kinds. On the one hand, they come from the human person *as human* or as constituted in such a species; let us call them "connatural" to man and specifically human. On the other hand, they come from the human person *insofar as he is a person* or participating in that transcendental perfection that is personality and which is realized in God infinitely better than in us. Let us call them then "transnatural" and metaphysical aspirations.

The connatural aspirations tend to a relative freedom compatible with conditions here below, and the burden of material nature inflicts upon them from the very beginning a serious defeat because no animal is born more naked and less free than man. The struggle to win freedom in the order of social life aims to make up for this defeat.

The transnatural aspirations of the person in us seek superhuman freedom, pure and simple freedom. And to whom belongs such freedom if not to Him alone who is freedom of independence itself, subsistent by itself? Man has no right to the freedom proper to God. When he aspires by a transnatural desire to this freedom, he seeks it in an "inefficacious" manner and without even knowing what it is. Thus divine transcendence imposes immediately the admission of a profound defeat on the part of these metaphysical aspirations of the person in us. However, such a defeat is not irreparable, at least if the victor descends to the aid of the vanquished. The movement to win freedom in the order of spiritual life aims precisely to make up for this defeat. But we must not hide from ourselves the fact that the point at which our reflection has now arrived is a crucial one for the human being. The least error here costs dearly. At this point capital errors, mortal for human society and the human soul, are mixed with capital truths to which are bound the life of the soul and that of society. We must work as hard as possible to distinguish truths from errors. There is a false conquest of freedom which is illusory and homicidal. There is a true conquest of freedom which provides truth and life for mankind.

In order to try to dissociate briefly one from the other, let me say that the false manner of understanding the attainment of freedom is based upon a philosophy called in technical language "univocalist" and "immanentist." In such a philosophy the notion of independence and freedom admits of neither internal variety nor degrees; and on the other hand God, if He exists, is conceived as a physical agent magnified *ad infinitum;* hence either He is considered *transcendent* and His *existence* is denied because He would be, as Proudhon believed, a sort of heavenly Tyrant imposing constraint and violence on everything other than Himself; or, on the other hand, His *existence* is affirmed and His *transcendence* is denied—all things are considered in the manner of Spinoza or Hegel as modes or phases of His realization. In this way of thinking, there is neither freedom nor autonomy except insofar as no objective rule or measure is received from a being other than oneself. And the human person claims for itself then divine freedom, so that man takes, in atheistic forms of thought and culture, the place of the God he denies, or man, through pantheistic forms, tries to realize in act an identity of nature with the God he imagines.

On the contrary, the true manner of understanding the attainment of freedom is based upon a philosophy of the analogy of being and divine transcendence. For this philosophy independence and freedom are realized, on the various levels of being, in several forms which are essentially diverse: in God in an absolute manner, and because (being supereminently all things) He is supreme interiority, of which all existing things are a participation; in us in a relative manner, and thanks to the privileges of the spirit which, however profound may be the state of dependence in which it is placed by the very nature of things, makes itself independent by its own operation when it poses interiorly to itself by knowledge and love the law it obeys. In such a philosophy divine transcendence imposes no violence nor constraint upon creatures, but rather infuses them with goodness and spontaneity and is more internal to them than they are to themselves. It is not true that the autonomy of an intelligent creature consists in not receiving any rule or objective measure from a being other than itself. It consists in conforming to such rules and measures voluntarily because they are known to be just and true, and because of a love for truth and justice. Such is human freedom, properly speaking, to which the person tends as towards a connatural perfection; and if the person aspires also to superhuman freedom, this thirst for a transnatural perfection, whose satisfaction is not due us, will be fully quenched only by the reception of more than is desired, and thanks to a transforming union with the Uncreated Nature. God is free from all eternity; more exactly, He is subsistent Freedom. Man is not born free save in the basic potencies of his being: he becomes free, by warring upon himself and thanks to many sorrows; by the struggle of the spirit and virtue; by exercising his freedom he wins his freedom. So that at long last a freedom better than he expected is *given* him. From the beginning to the end it is truth that liberates him.

TRUE AND FALSE POLITICAL EMANCIPATION

The first problem of vital importance evoked by the preceding considerations may be called the problem of true and false political emancipation. In fact, the conquest of freedom in the social and political order is the central hope characterizing the historical ideal of the last two centuries, and constituting at the same time its dynamic urge, and its power both of truth and of illusion. What I call false political emancipation is the philosophy and the social and political practice (and the corresponding emotional orchestration) based upon the false manner of understanding the conquest of freedom that I have briefly discussed. Necessarily this engenders myths that devour the human substance. What I call true political emancipation is the philosophy and the social and political practice (and the corresponding emotional orchestration) based upon the true manner of understanding the conquest of freedom. This leads to no myth but to a concrete historical ideal and to a patient labor of forming and educating the human substance.

The misfortune in the eyes of the philosopher of culture is the fact that the great democratic movements of modern times, especially in Europe, have so often sought true political emancipation under false standards, that is, under the standards of a general philosophy which is forgetful of the Gospel inspiration from which the democratic impulse proceeds and from which it is in reality inseparable, at least with respect to the actual movement of life if not to the systems of the theoreticians. In the obscure work which takes place in the hearts of men and in their history, a treasury of aspirations, efforts, and social realizations, achieved sometimes at the price of heroic sacrifices and originally directed towards the true conquest of freedom, has been conceptualized in the metaphysics of the false conquest of freedom; and to the extent that this work has been thus corrupted and deformed by a false philosophy of life, it is accompanied by errors and destructions which tend to the negation of its own vital principle and which finally make the democratic ideal seem to many minds an imposture. The totalitarian catastrophe which has let loose its hell upon Europe gives testimony of the immense gravity of this historical phenomenon. If the true city of human rights, the true democracy, does not succeed in freeing itself from the false and in triumphing over an anti-democratic enslavement; if in the ordeal of fire and blood a radical purification is not brought about, Western civilization risks entering upon a night without end. If we are confident that this will not happen, it is because we are confident that the necessary renovations will occur.

For the sake of further clarification, let me say briefly that the false political emancipation (the false city of human rights) has as its principle the "anthropocentric" conception that Rousseau and Kant had of the autonomy of the person. According to them, man is free *only if he obeys himself alone,* and man is constituted by right of nature in such a state of freedom (which Rousseau considered as lost owing to the corruption involved in social life and which Kant relegated to the noumenal world). In a word; we have here a divinization of the individual, the logical consequences of which are, in the practical and social order: (1) a practical atheism in society (for there is no place for two gods in the world, and if the individual is in practice god, God is no longer God except perhaps in a decorative way and for private use); (2) the theoretical and practical disappearance of the idea of the common good; (3) the theoretical and practical disappearance of the idea of the responsible leader, and of the idea of authority falsely considered to be incompatible with freedom: and this in the political sphere (where the possessors of authority should direct men not towards the private good of other men but towards the common good) as well as in the sphere of labor and of economics (where the technical exigencies of production demand that men work, in extremely diverse ways and proportions, for the private good of other men while at the same time making their own living). By virtue of an inevitable internal dialectic this social divinization of the individual, inaugurated by bourgeois liberalism, leads to the social divinization of the State and of the anonymous mass incarnate in a Master who is no longer a normal ruler but a sort of inhuman monster whose omnipotence is based upon myths and lies; and at the same time bourgeois liberalism makes way for revolutionary totalitarianism.

True political emancipation, on the contrary, or the true city of human rights, has as its principle a conception of the autonomy of the person in conformity with the nature of things and therefore "theocentric." According to this notion, obedience accepted for justice's sake is not opposed to freedom. It is, on the contrary, a normal way of arriving at freedom. Man must gradually win a freedom which consists, in the political and social order, above all in becoming, under given historical conditions, as independent as possible of the restrictions of material nature. In short, the human person transcends the earthly society of which he is a member inasmuch as he is made for God and for participation in absolute goods, but to the extent that he owes to society what he is, he is part of society as of a whole which is greater and better than he.

Thus the true city of human rights recognizes as God only one God: God Himself and no created thing. And this city understands that human society, despite the diverse religious families living within it, implies a religious principle and presupposes that God is accessible to our reason and is the last end of our existence. This city is founded upon the authentic notion of the common good—which is something different from a collection of private goods, but which demands to flow back upon individual persons; it implies the effective respect for their rights and has as its essential element their access to the maximum development and freedom compatible with given historical conditions. And finally, this city implies an authentic notion of authority.

For the true city of human rights, the possessors of authority in the political sphere are, in a democratic regime, designated by the people. They govern the people by virtue of this designation and under the regulating control of the people ("government of the people, by the people"), and for the common good of the people ("government for the people"). But they really have the right to command; and they command free persons each of whom is called to participate concretely, in the greatest possible measure, in political life, and who are not abandoned like atoms, but rather are grouped in organic communities beginning with the family, which forms the basic natural community.

In the sphere of labor and economic relations the true city

of human rights demands that the constant development of social justice compensate for the restrictions imposed upon man by the necessities (in themselves not human but technical) of the work to be done and the production to be realized. This city knows that to serve the private good of another man and become to this extent his tool is in itself an affliction for the radical aspirations of personality, but it also knows that this is a condition imposed upon men by material nature, a condition over which the progress of conscience and of society must someday triumph here below, although this triumph will be perfect only in the land of the resurrected. This true city of human rights demands that, by a persevering struggle for improvement due at once to the perfection and extension of mechanical equipment and to the tension of spiritual energies transforming secular life from within, the conditions of work become less and less servile and tend to a state of real deliverance for the human person. At the present stage of historical development, it would seem that for certain types of workers this result can be obtained to a remarkable degree—after the crisis which the world is suffering today has brought about a reformation of the structures and the spirit of the economic order—not only by reducing the hours of work, but also by granting the workers co-ownership and co-management of the enterprise.

But here, as in the political sphere, the inauguration of new structures, no matter how important, does not suffice. The soul of social life is fashioned by that which superabounds in it from the true and proper life of individual persons, from the gift of self which that life involves, and from a gratuitous generosity whose source lies in the inmost part of the heart. More concisely, good will and a relation of respect and love between persons and between the person and the community can alone give to the life of the social body a truly human character. If the person has the opportunity of being treated as a person in social life, and if the unpleasant works which this life imposes can be made easy and happy and even exalting, it is first of all due to the development of law and to institutions of law. But it is also and indispensably due to the development of civic friendship, with the confidence and mutual devotion this implies on the part of those who carry it out. For the true city of human rights, fraternity is not a privilege of nature which flows from the natural goodness of man and which the State need only proclaim. It is the end of a slow and difficult conquest which demands virtue and sacrifice and a perpetual victory of man over himself. In this sense, we can say that the heroic ideal towards which true political emancipation tends is the inauguration of a fraternal city. It is seen here how, in fact, true political emancipation depends on the Christian ferment deposited in the world and presupposes finally, as its most profound stimulus, evangelical love exalting things of earthly civilization in their proper order.

The properties that I have just sketched were not absent from the democratic movement and hopes of modern times. They characterize, on the contrary, what was unconsciously exercised most profoundly and vitally in it. But this good seed was preyed upon and vitiated by a philosophy of false political emancipation, and the monsters engendered by the latter threaten by an implacable dialectic to smother the authentic seed. We thus have a presentiment of the vast purifications and renovations referred to above.

THE TRUE AND FALSE DEIFICATION OF MAN

There is a true and false emancipation in the political and social order. In the spiritual order there is a true and false deification of man. This is another problem of vital importance, fundamental and absolutely primary, posed by the natural instinct which impels man to win freedom.

As I have said at the beginning of this essay, by the fact that we participate in the transcendental perfection desig-

nated by the word "personality," we have within us transnatural aspirations the satisfaction of which is not due us in
justice but which nevertheless torment us and tend to a superhuman freedom, freedom pure and simple—that is to say,
to a divine freedom. Evidence of these aspirations for the
superhuman, these desires to reach the borders of divinity,
has been presented by the sages of all times.

The great spiritual errors also bear witness to these aspirations. They seek the deification of man, but by man's own
forces and the development of the powers of his nature only.
More often they take a pantheistic form, as can be seen in
the gnostic currents of former times, in the great monistic
metaphysics, and in the mysticism of quietism. It was left,
however, to modern times to look for the deification of man
by doing away with wisdom and breaking with God. Historically, in my opinion, the two main sources of this false
deification are: (1) The immanentist conception of conscience which since the Lutheran revolution has gradually
gained the ascendancy, and which demands that what is
within man—"my interior freedom"—construct morality by
itself alone without owing anything to law. (2) The idealist
conception of science which since the Cartesian revolution
has gradually gained the ascendancy and which demands
that what is within man—"my self or my spirit"—construct
truth by itself alone without owing anything to things. Hy-
perspiritualist as they first seem, these two conceptions make
science independent of being, and conscience independent
of law, and claim for that which is within man the kind of
independence proper to God. In reality these two erroneous
conceptions materialize the human soul and plunge it into
external action, where by seeking its proper and only mode of
realization it becomes the slave of time, matter, and the
world. Science finally will be subjugated by a kind of demi-
urgic imperialism applied to enslave material nature to the
lusts of human beings. Conscience too will be subjugated by
a kind of demonic imperialism applied to "oppose oneself" in

order to "pose oneself," following the phrase of Fichte, and to realize oneself by dominating others. Man, become the god of this world, will believe that he will find divine freedom for himself by being independent of God, and consequently by the radical negation of God. The false deification of man will take the atheistic form which appears in our day in an amazingly barbarous light.

It made its first appearance in the disguised atheism of orthodox Kantianism and bourgeois liberalism. After the bankruptcy of this atheism which found religion "good for the people," and after the failure of the false individualistic conquest of freedom and personality, it was inevitable that the false deification of man be affirmed by the patent atheism of Marxist Hegelianism, which sees in religion "the opium of the people," or the perverted paganism of racism, which reduces religion to the idolatry of the "soul of the people." Plebeian totalitarianism, either under the Soviet Communist or German Nazi form, then undertakes to lead collective man by war, forced labor, and the standardization of souls to the achievement of freedom. Inevitably, from the moment that absolute freedom, emancipation pure and simple, divine independence were sought in the human itself, or in other words, from the moment that the *transnatural* aspirations of the person were lowered into the sphere of *connatural* aspirations—and by that very fact perverted and made infinite—the social was to become deified, the things of Caesar were to absorb monstrously the things of God, and the pagan empire was to make itself adored.

On the contrary, the transnatural aspirations of the human person tend normally towards God, the transcendental cause of being, and they incite the soul to seek liberation in Him. Despite all its imperfections and blemishes, such was the *élan* of the great Hellenic wisdom. In Hindu spirituality, however, at least if its proliferation, at times poisonous, is reduced to what is most pure in it, are found the most significant examples of states to which these *transnatural* aspirations can lead man when by his own action and the ascetic use of his natural powers he turns his own nature back against itself. I think that what in Christian language we call the "natural" mystical experience and the highest "natural" contemplation then reaches by way of an entirely intellectual self-annihilation the substance of the Self, and through and in it the divine Omnipresence.[2] This is a liberation and deliverance at one and the same time ultimate in the order of what nature is capable of, and not ultimate, absolutely speaking, in regard to our real destiny and its hidden primordial truth that nature has been made for grace. Hence this conquest of spiritual freedom is ambivalent: true and authentic on its plane if the soul does not stop there and it opens itself to the highest gifts; false and deceptive if the soul stops there or if it looks upon it as a necessary means, or if it takes it for deification.

There is, however, a true deification of man. *Ego dixi: dii estis.* This is called eternal life—which begins obscurely here on earth. It is as fatal to renounce perfect liberation as it is to try to reach it by the wrong ways, that is to say, by oneself alone. The transnatural aspirations are supernaturally fulfilled, and by a gift which surpasses anything we can conceive. What is grace, the theologians ask, if not a formal participation in the Divine Nature, in other words, a deifying life received from God?

The mystery of this is that the supreme freedom and independence of man are won by the supreme spiritual realization of his dependence, his dependence on a Being who being Life itself vivifies, and being Freedom itself, liberates all who participate in His essence. This kind of dependence is not one of external constraint, as is the case of one physical agent in regard to another physical agent. The more he realizes it the more does man participate in the nature of the

<hr/>

[2] See my book *Quatre Essais sur l'Esprit dans sa Condition Charnelle,* Chapter III; *Ransoming the Time* (New York: Charles Scribner's Sons, 1941), Chapter X, "The Natural Mystical Experience and the Void."

Absolute. Men who have become something of God participate in the freedom of Him who cannot be contained by
anything. By losing themselves they have won a mysterious
and disappropriated personality which makes them act by
virtue of that which they are eternally in the Uncreated Essence. Born of spirit they are free like it. To tell the truth,
they have won nothing, and they have received all. While
they worked and suffered to attain freedom, it gave itself to
them. The true conquest of supreme and absolute freedom
is to be made free by Subsistent Freedom and to consent
freely to it. The true deification of man consists in opening
himself to the gift which the Absolute makes of Itself, and
the descent of the divine plenitude into the intelligent
creature.

What I am saying is that this is all the work of love. Law
protects and fosters freedom. When love follows the path of
law it leads through law to emancipation from all servitude,
even the servitude of the law. I have often quoted, and I
wish to quote again, the text from the *Summa contra Gentiles* where St. Thomas comments on St. Paul, which I regard as one of the great texts absolutely fundamental for the
spiritual constitution of humanity.

We must observe that the sons of God are led by the divine
Spirit, not as though they were slaves, but as being free. For,
since to be free is to be cause of one's own actions, we are said
to do freely what we do of ourselves. Now this is what we do willingly: and what we do unwillingly, we do, not freely but under
compulsion. This compulsion may be absolute, when the cause is
wholly extraneous, and the patient contributes nothing to the action, for instance, when a man is compelled to move by force; or
it may be partly voluntary, as when a man is willing to do or suffer that which is less opposed to his will, in order to avoid that
which is more opposed thereto. Now, the sanctifying Spirit inclines us to act, in such a way as to make us act willingly, inasmuch as He causes us to be lovers of God. Hence the sons of God
are led by the Holy Ghost to act freely and for love, not slavishly

and for fear: wherefore the Apostle says [Rom. 8:15]: *"You have not received the Spirit of bondage again in fear; but you have received the spirit of adoption of sons."*

Now the will is by its essence directed to that which is truly good: so that when, either through passion or through an evil habit or disposition, a man turns away from what is truly good, he acts slavishly, in so far as he is led by something extraneous, *if we consider the natural direction of the will;* but if we consider the act of the will, as *inclined here and now towards an apparent good,* he acts freely when he follows the passion or evil habit, but he acts slavishly if, while his will remains the same, he refrains from what he desires through fear of the law which forbids the fulfillment of his desire. Accordingly, when the divine Spirit by love inclines the will to the true good to which it is naturally directed, He removes both the servitude [the heteronomy, as we would say today] whereby a man, the slave of passion and sin, acts against the order of the will, and the servitude whereby a man acts against the inclination of his will, and in obedience to the law, as the slave and not the friend of the law. Wherefore the Apostle says [II Cor. 3:17]: *"Where the Spirit of the Lord is, there is liberty,"* and [Gal. 5:18]: *"If you are led by the Spirit you are not under the law."*[3]

Great is the distance between the imperfect liberation whereby the highest techniques of natural spirituality oblige nature to satisfy in some way the transnatural aspirations of the human person, and the perfect freedom whereby the supernatural gift that the Divine Personality makes of Itself to the created personality more than fulfills these aspirations. While leaving intact the distinction of natures, love, which at the end of spiritual growth creates this perfect freedom, also makes man a god by participation. At the same time, far from enclosing itself in an altogether intellectual contemplation which would do away with action, the freedom we have in mind lives by a contemplation which, since it proceeds from love, superabounds in action and penetrates to that

[3] St. Thomas Aquinas, *Summa contra Gentiles,* IV, 22.

which is most intimate in the world. The heroism it implies does not retreat into the sacred; it spills over into the profane and sanctifies it. Detached from perfection in perfection itself, because it wants more to love than to be without fault, it awakens, more and more, good will and brotherly love.

To return to the distinction between the socio-temporal and the spiritual, the things which belong to Caesar and those which belong to God, I should point out, finally, that the false deification of man results, as we have seen, in the confusion of the temporal and the spiritual, and in a perverse adoration of the social and temporal relativities erected into an absolute; conversely, the true deification of man, because it is accomplished by the grace of the Incarnation and draws to itself all that is human, demands of divine things that they descend into the most profound depths of the human, and insists that the political and social order, while remaining essentially distinct from the spiritual, be pervaded and intrinsically superelevated by the sap which flows into souls from the Absolute. In the degree, small as it may be in fact, that things are this way, in that degree the historical march of civilization towards the conquest of relative freedom, which responds to the *connatural* aspirations of human personality, is in accord and in mutual concourse with the suprahistorical movement of the soul towards the conquest of absolute freedom, which responds, by transcending them divinely, to the *transnatural* aspirations of the person as a person.

APPENDIX A

EDUCATION FOR THE GOOD LIFE

The problems of Modern Education, or rather of postwar education, are as many-faceted as they are serious and urgent. . . . I would say briefly that the great achievements of modern and progressive education in the psychologic and pedagogic field, its generous effort toward a better understanding of the needs of youth, toward more living and less bookish methods, and toward a better preparation for real life in the social community, have been preyed upon and seriously imperiled by the positivist, empiricist, agnostic and pragmatist philosophies which give themselves as the standard-bearers of the new education, while overlooking both what man is and what dignity and primacy truth, the intellect and the creative powers of the human soul possess and claim by nature.

The crucial need for modern education is to free itself from the background of this philosophy, which is but a hindrance to its inspiration and which takes the edge off the sense of truth and off the eternal values of our minds.

In a more general way the great industrial or technological revolution, which is decidedly taking the upper hand today all over the world, places mankind before a momentous choice: either the new age of civilization will yield to matter and technocracy and will give up the historic mission of the human race to achieve freedom and advance toward a culture and a social regime dedicated to human brotherhood, or else the wonderful means put at our disposal by technology and the new social structures which are in the making will be used for the liberation of man and for a real improvement, both material and spiritual, of human life. But the very choice of that road of real progress and emancipation will indispensably require that the new age of civilization abandon in all fields, and especially in the field of education, a philosophy of life which disarms and jeopardizes the highest powers of man, and that it find anew, in a heroic manner, faith in truth, in reason, and in God.

We are waging today a war of civilization. What we are fighting for is human dignity, justice, freedom, law, the eternal call which makes every human person worthy of respect and love, and the openness of the future to liberating and fraternal work. All of these things are rooted in the moral and spiritual order. What is our faith in those things? What is our certainty that they are actually true—true to the point that we can die for them—and that reason—reason relying on its own powers, and reason enlightened by Christian faith—is able to demonstrate their validity? The great predicament of the democracies is the fact that they had lost intellectual faith in the truths that constitute their very soul and their very principles. The particular mistakes which they may have made before this war were incomparably less important than the general ignorance of what they wanted, of the ends to which their will had to be determined; and such an ignorance could be ascribed to their general skepticism about the moral and spiritual realities without which democracy is nothing but nonsense.

If we are to overcome this predicament, our intellect must seize hold of these realities. In other words, what we need first of all is a renewal both of metaphysics and of morality, backed up by faith in the Gospel. This is true in the general field of culture; it is especially true in the field of education.

APPENDIX B

THE CRUCIAL PROBLEM OF THE EDUCATION
OF THE HUMAN BEING

Such are . . . the two metaphysical aspects of the human being: individuality and personality, each with their own ontological physiognomy. Let us note, that we do not represent two separate things. There is not in me one reality called my individuality and another called my personality. It is the same entire being which, in one sense, is an individual and, in another sense, a person. I am wholly an individual, by reason of what I receive from matter, and I am wholly a person, by reason of what I receive from spirit; just as a painting is in its entirety a physico-chemical complex, by reason of the coloring materials out of which it is made, and a work of beauty, by reason of the painter's art.

Let us note, moreover, that material individuality is not something bad in itself. No, it is not something bad in itself. No, it is something good, since it is the very condition of our existence. But it is precisely in relation to personality that individuality is good; what is bad, is to let this aspect of our being predominate in our actions. No doubt, each of my acts is an act of myself-the-individual and an act of myself-the-person. But even as it is free and engages my whole self, each of my acts is drawn *either* into the movement which tends to the supreme center toward which personality strives, *or* into the movement which tends toward dispersion, to which, if left to itself, material individuality is bound to fall back.

Now it is important to observe that man must complete, through his own will, what is sketched in his nature. According to a commonplace expression, which is a very profound one, man must become what he is. In the moral order, he must win, by himself, his freedom and his personality. In other words, his action can follow either the slope of personality or the slope of individuality. If the development of the human being follows the direction of *material individuality,* he will be carried in the direction of the "hateful ego," whose law is to *snatch,* to absorb for oneself. In this case, personality as such will tend to adulterate, to dissolve. If, on the contrary, the development follows the direction of *spiritual personality,* then it will be in the direction of the generous self of saints and heroes that man will be carried. Man will really be a person, insofar as the life of spirit and of freedom will dominate in him that of passion and the senses.

Here we stand before the crucial problem of the education of the human being. Certain educators confuse person and individual; in order to grant personality the development and the freedom of expansion to which it aspires, they refuse all asceticism, they want man to yield fruit without being pruned. They think that the happiness of man consists in that joyous smile which is seen, in the advertisements, on the faces of boys and girls relishing a good cigarette or a glass of Coca-Cola. Instead of fulfilling himself, man disperses and disassociates himself. The heart atrophies itself and the senses are exasperated. Or, in other cases, what is most human in man falls back into a kind of vacuity, which is covered by frivolity.

And there are other educators and rulers who misunderstand the distinction of person and individual. They mistake it for a separation. They think that we bear in ourselves two separate beings, that of the individual and that of the person. And, according to these educators: *Death to the individual! Long live the person!* Unfortunately, when one kills the individual, one also kills the person. The *despotic* conception of the progress of the human being is no better than the *anarchic* one. The ideal of this despotic conception is first to take out our heart, with anaesthetics if possible, and next to replace it by the heart of an angel. The second operation is more difficult than the first one, and is but rarely successful. Instead of the authentic person, imprinted with the mysterious face of the Creator, there appears a mask, the austere mask of the Pharisee.

In reality, what is especially important for the education and the progress of the human being, in the moral and spiritual order (as well as in the order of organic growth), is the interior principle, that is to say, nature and grace. The right educational means are but auxiliaries; the art, a co-operating art, at the service of this interior principle. And the entire art consists in cutting off and in pruning—both in the case of the person, the weight of individuality should diminish, and that of real personality and of its generosity, should increase. And this, indeed, is far from easy.

BIBLIOGRAPHY

For a complete bibliography of the works by and about Jacques Maritain, see *The Achievement of Jacques and Raïssa Maritain: A Bibliography 1906–1961,* by Donald and Idella Gallagher (New York: Doubleday & Company, 1962).

I. *Texts Included in this Volume*

"Preface" to *Philosophy and Education,* by Frans de Hovre (New York: Benziger Brothers, 1930), pp. v–xi.
Translation of the preface to *Essai de philosophie pédagogique* (Brussels: Albert DeWit, 1927).
"Thomist Views on Education," in *Modern Philosophies and Education,* edited by Nelson B. Henry (Chicago: University of Chicago Press, 1955), pp. 57–90. (See Section II for French version.)
"Education and the Humanities" (Centenary Lecture delivered in the Fall of 1952 at St. Michael's College, Toronto, Canada).
"Moral and Spiritual Values in Education," *Proceedings of the Eighty-ninth Convocation of the Board of Regents of the State of New York* (April 25, 1958), pp. 14–21.
"Moral Education," in *A College Goes to School: Centennial Lectures* (Notre Dame-Holy Cross, Indiana: St. Mary's College; and Paterson, New Jersey: St. Anthony's Guild Press, 1945), pp. 1–25.
"Some Typical Aspects of Christian Education," in *The Christian Idea of Education,* edited by Edmund Fuller (New Haven: Yale University Press, 1957), pp. 173–198. (This essay appears in French in *Nova et Vetera,* XXXI, 1956, pp. 1–25).
"The Education of Women," taken from Address in *The Inauguration of George N. Shuster, the Fifth President* (New

York: Hunter College of the City of New York, 1941), pp. 31–36.

"The Conquest of Freedom," in *Freedom: Its Meaning*, planned and edited by Ruth Nanda Anshen (New York: Harcourt, Brace & Company, 1940), pp. 631–649. (Appears in French in *Principes d'une politique humaniste*. New York: Éditions de la Maison Française, 1944, premier chapitre.)

"Education for the Good Life," taken from *The Commonweal*, XLIV, (April 23, 1946). See below.

"The Crucial Problem of the Education of the Human Being," taken from *Scholasticism and Politics*, by Jacques Maritain (New York: The Macmillan Company, 1954), pp. 52–54.

II. *Other Works on Education by Jacques Maritain*

Education at the Crossroads (New Haven: Yale University Press, 1943). Pp. x, 120. Paperback edition, Yale University Press, 1960.

French translation: L'Éducation à la Croisée des Chemins (Paris: Egloff, 1947). Pp. 239. Contains special appendix on "Le problème de l'école publique en France." This book was also translated into Portuguese, Italian, Spanish, German and Japanese.

Pour une Philosophie de l'Éducation (Paris: Librairie Arthème Fayard, 1959). Pp. 249.

This work includes "L'Éducation à la croisée des chemins," "Vues thomistes sur l'éducation," "Sur quelques aspects typiques de l'éducation chrétienne," and "Le problème de l'école publique en France."

"On Teaching," in *The Catholic Layman: On Teaching* (Toronto: St. Michael's College, 1933), pp. 9–12. (No. 1 of the Pamphlet.)

"Education at the Crossroads," in *Great Issues in Education* (Chicago: The Great Books Foundation, 1956), Volume II, pp. 117–151. (Selections from *Education at the Crossroads*.)

"Education for Tomorrow," *The Yale Review*, XXXII (June, 1943), pp. 670–680. (From *Education at the Crossroads*.)

"Education for the Good Life," *The Commonweal*, XLIV (April 23, May 3, and May 10, 1946), pp. 36–40, 68–70, 90–92. (From *Education at the Crossroads.*)

"Higher Learning and Unity," *The Commonweal*, XXXVIII (July 9, 1943), pp. 290–293. (From *Education at the Crossroads.*)

"Les humanités," *Mercure de France*, CCC (July, 1947), pp. 435–446. (From *L'Éducation à la Croisée des Chemins.*)

"Convocation Address," *Academic Convocation Commemorating the Tercentenary of the Birth of St. John Baptist de la Salle* (New York: Manhattan College, 1951), pp. 15–19.

III. *Books and Articles on Maritain's Educational Philosophy*

Beales, A. C. F. "Jacques Maritain," in *The Function of Teaching: Seven Approaches to Purpose, Tradition and Environment*, edited by A. V. Judges. London: Faber & Faber, 1959, pp. 67–88.

Cassata, Maria Letizia. *La pedagogia di Jacques Maritain*. Palermo: Tipografia "Boccone del Povero," 1953. Pp. 103.

Counts, George S. "The Liberal Tradition in Education," *Survey-Graphic*, XXXII (December, 1943), pp. 508–509.

Elia, Sílvio. "Maritain e o questão pedagógica," *A Ordem*, XXXV (Maritain Issue of May–June 1946), pp. 570–575.

Endslow, B. S. "Educational Theories of Jacques Maritain," *The Catholic Educational Review*, I (March, 1952), pp. 191–192. (Abstract of M.A. thesis written for the Catholic University of America.)

Farrell, Allan P. "Bending the Twig," *America*, LXXI (August 19, 1944), pp. 499–500.

Fecher, Charles A. "The Philosophy of Education," in *The Philosophy of Jacques Maritain*. Westminster, Maryland: The Newman Press, 1953, pp. 275–285.

Gallagher, Donald A. "Future of Education—Specialization or Wisdom?" *The Catholic Worker*, XIII (September, 1946), pp. 1, 2, and 7.

Greene, T. M. "The Mind of Maritain," *The Yale Review*, XXXIII (Winter 1944), pp. 377–383.

O'Malley, Frank. "Education of Man: A Discussion of *Education at the Crossroads,* by Jacques Maritain," *The Review of Politics,* VI (January, 1944), pp. 3–17.

Ramon-Fernandez, Irène. "Deux philosophies de l'éducation: Newman et Maritain," *Recherches et Débats,* VIII (1954), pp. 50–66.

Tead, Ordway. "Education and God," *The Saturday Review of Literature,* XXVII (April 22, 1944), pp. 24–25.

Tierney, M. "M. Maritain on Education," *Studies,* XXXIII (March, 1944), pp. 21–29.

Viotto, Piero. "Il messaggio educativo di Maritain," in *Pedagogia della Persona,* by Marco Agosti and others. Brescia: La Scuola, 1952.

Ward, Leo R. "Maritain on Education for Freedom," *Proceedings of The American Catholic Philosophical Association,* XXX (1956), pp. 154–159.

IV. *Recommended Readings in Education*[*]

Adler, Mortimer J. "Adult Education," *Journal of Higher Education,* XXII (February, 1952).

Adler, Mortimer J. "Character and Intelligence," in *A College Goes to School: Centennial Lectures.* Notre Dame-Holy Cross, Indiana: St. Mary's College; and Paterson, New Jersey: St. Anthony Guild Press, 1945.

Adler, Mortimer J. "The Order of Learning," *Moraga Quarterly* (Autumn, 1941). St. Mary's College, California.

Adler, Mortimer J. "Liberalism and Liberal Education," *Educational Record,* XX (July, 1939), pp. 422–436.

Adler, Mortimer J. "Seminar on Education in a Modern Industrial Democracy" (Philadelphia, June 19 and 20, 1952). Unpublished.

Barr, Stringfellow. *Report of the President.* Annapolis, Maryland: St. John's College, July, 1942.

Benedict, Agnes. *Progress to Freedom.* New York: G. P. Putnam's Sons, 1942.

Boyle, George. *Father Tompkins of Nova Scotia.* New York: P. J. Kenedy & Sons, 1953.

[*] The following list of books on education was prepared by Professor Maritain as a supplement to "Thomist Views on Education."

Brameld, Theodore. *Patterns of Educational Philosophy.* Yonkers-on-Hudson, New York: World Book Company, 1950. Revised.

Brubacher, John S. *Modern Philosophies of Education.* New York and London: McGraw-Hill Book Company, 1950.

Cairns, Huntington. "The Humanities and the Law," *New York University Law Review* (January, 1952).

Chambers, Gordon Keith. *The Republic and the Person.* Chicago: Henry Regnery Company, 1952.

Clarke, Fred, et al. *A Review of Educational Thought.* London: University of London Institute of Education, 1942.

Cohen, I. Bernard. "The Education of the Public in Science," *Impact of Science on Society* (Summer, 1952).

Conant, James Bryant. *Education and Liberty.* Cambridge, Massachusetts: Harvard University Press, 1953.

Cunningham, William F. *The Pivotal Problems of Education.* New York: Macmillan Company, 1940.

Cunningham, William F. *General Education and the Liberal College.* St. Louis, Missouri: B. Herder Book Company, 1953.

Dodds, Harold W. "To Teach Wisdom," *Princeton Alumni Weekly* (May 9, 1952). (Address at the National Alumni Association Banquet, Chicago, April 25, 1952.)

Durand, Suzanne Marie. *Pour ou contre l'Éducation nouvelle,* Paris: Desclée de Brouwer, 1951.

Elkin, Daniel C. "A Case for the Study of the Humanities in the Making of a Doctor," *Annals of Surgery,* LXVII (September, 1952).

General Education in a Free Society. Report of the Harvard Committee. Cambridge, Massachusetts: Harvard University Press, 1945.

Gilson, Etienne. *The Breakdown of Morals and Christian Education.* Toronto: St. Michael's College, 1952.

Hutchins, Robert M. *Education for Freedom.* Baton Rouge, Louisiana: Louisiana State University Press, 1943.

Hutchins, Robert M. *The Higher Learning in America.* New Haven: Yale University Press, 1936.

Hutchins, Robert M. *No Friendly Voice.* Chicago: University of Chicago Press, 1936.

Marrou, Henri. *Histoire de l'Éducation dans l'Antiquité*. Paris: Éditions du Seuil, 1948. English translation: Sheed & Ward, 1956.

Meiklejohn, Alexander. *Education Between Two Worlds*. New York: Harper & Bros., 1942.

Montessori, Maria. *The Montessori Method*. New York: Frederick A. Stokes, 1912.

Montessori, Maria. *Pedagogical Anthropology*. New York: Frederick A. Stokes, 1913.

Nef, John U. *The Universities Look for Unity*. New York: Pantheon, 1943.

Nef, John U. "The University of Chicago and the World, 1929–1951," *The Review of Politics*, XLI (October 1951).

Newman, John Henry. *The Idea of a University Defined and Illustrated*. London, New York and Bombay: Longmans, Green & Company, 1901. Paperback Edition: Rinehart & Company, 1960.

Newman, John Henry. *On the Scope and Nature of University Education*. New York: E. P. Dutton & Co., 1915.

Nicholson, Marjorie Hope. *Newton Demands the Muse*. Princeton, New Jersey: Princeton University Press, 1946.

Oates, Whitney J. "The Humanities: A Philosophic Background" (Chicago Conference on the Humanities, April, 1952), in *Princeton Alumni Weekly*, May 9, 1952.

Piaget, Jean. *The Child's Conception of the World*. New York: Harcourt, Brace & Co., 1929.

Piaget, Jean. *Judgment and Reasoning in the Child*. New York: Harcourt, Brace & Co., 1928.

Piaget, Jean. *The Origins of Intelligence in Children*. New York: International Universities Press, 1952.

Polanyi, Michael. *Physical Science and Human Values*. Princeton, New Jersey: Princeton University Press, 1946.

Tate, Allen. "The Man of Letters in the Modern World," *The Forlorn Demon*. Chicago: Henry Regnery Company, 1953.

Taylor, Hugh S. *Religious Perspectives of College Teaching in the Physical Sciences*. New Haven, Connecticut: Edward W. Hazen Foundation, n.d.

Viner, Jacob. *A Modest Proposal for Some Stress on Scholarship in Graduate Training*. Princeton, New Jersey: Princeton University Press, 1953.

Whitehead, Alfred N. *The Aims of Education and Other Essays*. New York: Macmillan & Co., 1929. Paperback Edition: Mentor Books, 1949.